The Poetry of Ted Hughes

DATE DUE

14. SEP 2005			
17. JAN 2006			
FEB 2008			

WITHDRAWN

GAYLORD			PRINTED IN U S A

Studies in Twentieth-Century Literature

Series Editor:
Stan Smith, Professor of English, University of Dundee

Published Titles:
Rainer Emig, *Modernism in Poetry: Motivations, Structures and Limits*
Lee Horsley, *Fictions of Power in English Literature: 1900–1950*
Peter Brooker, *New York Fiction: Modernity, Postmodernism,*
The New Modern
Richard Kirkland, *Literature and Culture in Northern Ireland Since 1965:*
Moments of Danger
Keith Williams and Steven Matthews (eds), *Rewriting the Thirties:*
Modernism and After
Paul Bentley, *The Poetry of Ted Hughes: Language, Illusion and Beyond*

The Poetry of Ted Hughes: Language, Illusion and Beyond

Paul Bentley

Longman
London and New York

Addison Wesley Longman
Edinburgh Gate
Harlow
Essex CM20 2JE
England
and Associated Companies throughout the world.

*Published in the United States of America
by Addison Wesley Longman Inc., New York.*

First published 1998

ISBN 0 582 22776 3 CSD
ISBN 0 582 22775 5 PPR

British Library Cataloguing-in-Publication Data

A catalogue record of this book is available
from the British Library

Library of Congress Cataloging-in-Publication Data

Ted Hughes / edited by Paul Bentley.
     p. cm. — (Studies in twentieth-century literature)
    Includes bibliographical references (p.   ) and index.
    ISBN 0–582–22776–3 (hardcover). — ISBN 0–582–22775–5 (pbk.)
    1. Hughes, Ted, 1930–   —Criticism and interpretation.
  I. Bentley, Paul. II. Series: Studies in twentieth-century
literature (Longman (Firm))
PR6058.U37Z897   1998
821'.914—dc21

                               97–20600
                                CIP

Set by 35 in 10/12 pt Bembo
Produced by Longman Singapore Publishers (Pte) Ltd.
Printed in Singapore

Contents

Contents

Acknowledgements

Thanks to Stan Smith and Neil Roberts.
Special thanks to Anne Charman.

The Publishers are grateful to the following for permission to reproduce copyright material:

Columbia University Press for extracts from *BLACK SUN* by Julia Kristeva. Copyright © 1992 by Columbia University Press; Faber & Faber Ltd. for extracts from 'The Chronological Order of Sylvia Plath's Poems' by Ted Hughes in Ted Newman's edition of *THE ART OF SYLVIA PLATH: A SYMPOSIUM* (Fabers, 1970) © Ted Hughes 1970. *CAVE BIRDS* by Ted Hughes (Fabers 1975) © Ted Hughes 1975. *THE CROW* by Ted Hughes (Fabers 1972) © 1972 by Ted Hughes. *FLOWERS AND INSECTS* by Ted Hughes (Fabers 1986) © Ted Hughes 1986. *GAUDETE* by Ted Hughes (Fabers 1977) © Ted Hughes 1977; *POETRY IN THE MAKING* by Ted Hughes (Fabers 1967) © Ted Hughes 1967. *RAIN CHARM FOR THE DUCHY AND OTHER LAUREATE POEMS* by Ted Hughes (Fabers 1992) © Ted Hughes 1992. *REMAINS OF ELMET* by Ted Hughes (Fabers 1979) © Ted Hughes 1979. 1986 *RIVER* by Ted Hughes (Fabers 1983) © Ted Hughes 1983; Faber & Faber Ltd./Farrar Straus & Giroux Inc. for extracts from *SHAKE-SPEARE AND THE GODDESS OF COMPLETE BEING* by Ted Hughes, (Fabers 1992/FSG 1992) © Ted Hughes 1992 and *WOLFWATCHING* by Ted Hughes (Fabers 1989/FSG 1991) © Ted Hughes 1991, 1992; Faber & Faber Ltd./ HarperCollins Inc. for extracts from *MOORTOWN/NEW SELECTED POEMS* by Ted Hughes (Fabers 1979/HarperCollins Inc. 1995). Copyright © 1979, 1982 by Ted Hughes. *REMAINS OF ELMET/NEW SELECTED POEMS* by Ted Hughes (Fabers 1979/HarperCollins Inc. 1995). Copyright © 1979, 1982 by Ted Hughes. *HAWK IN THE RAIN/SELECTED POEMS 1957–67* by Ted Hughes (Fabers 1957/HarperCollins Inc. 1995). Copyright © 1957, 1972 by Ted Hughes. Drawings copyright © 1973 by Harper & Row. *LUPERCAL/SELECTED POEMS 1957–67* by Ted Hughes (Fabers 1960/HarperCollins Inc. 1995). Copyright © 1960, 1972 by Ted Hughes. Drawings copyright © 1973 by Harper & Row. *WODWO/ SELECTED POEMS 1957–67* by Ted Hughes (Fabers 1967/HarperCollins Inc. 1995). Copyright © 1967, 1972 by Ted Hughes. Drawings copyright © 1973 by Harper & Row; Faber & Faber Ltd./St Martin's Press Inc. for extracts from *WINTER POLLEN* by Ted Hughes (Fabers 1994/St Martin's Press Inc. 1995) © Ted Hughes 1994, 1995.

To my mother

Introduction

This book had its conception in the feeling that a wealth of criticism on Ted Hughes has overlooked something, or rather, has not gone far enough in trying to account for it. This something is how the poet's language works, what makes the poems tick *as poems*, over and above what they appear to be saying. Hughes's poems are all too often read for their referential content: the word is taken to be transparent, a window onto what is being described or depicted (the world of nature, for example). The supposition is that Hughes's poems open out onto an extra-linguistic world of things and ideas — what linguists call signifieds, as distinct from the material part of the sign or word, its sound and written image: the signifier — and of course they do: if they did not the poems would be incomprehensible. This is the referential or mimetic aspect of the poems — their ability to body forth objects, animals, images and ideas. Yet at the same time as Hughes's poems refer outside themselves they also display a marked uneasiness (and by the same token playfulness) with language as a means of representation, more often than not calling attention to the act of representation itself, in other words, the creative act: it is as if the act of creating meaning is the significant thing here, over and above the signified meanings of the poems. In this sense Hughes's poems body forth not only animals and objects but also, more crucially, the materiality of their own medium. The reader is never allowed to forget that the materialization of a fox or a hawk in a Hughes poem is an act of language and imagination. This may seem a fairly elementary point to make, but its implications are far reaching. The illusion of reality here is an effect of language and imagination — or so the poems themselves seem to suggest.

It is in this insistent figuring of their own processes of coming-into-being that is to be found what is really at stake in Hughes's poems. What makes poetry poetry is that it does something with language that other forms of language use do not; it is Hughes's distinctive handling of language that is this book's primary concern. That is, the discussion privileges *language* over *theme*, or put another way, the *signifier* over the *signified*, with a view to bringing into sharp focus just what it is that makes a Hughes poem work.

HUGHES AND THE MOVEMENT

In 1956, a year before Hughes's first book of poems, *The Hawk in the Rain* (1957), appeared, Robert Conquest published an anthology of contemporary poetry called *New Lines*. In the introduction Conquest outlines the 'unity of approach, a new and healthy general standpoint' towards poetry that he finds in the work of the poets he represents (who thereafter came to be labelled as the Movement poets: the book includes selections from Philip Larkin, Kingsley Amis, D. J. Enright, Elizabeth Jennings and Donald Davie):

> If one had briefly to distinguish this poetry of the fifties from its predecessors, I believe the most important general point would be that it submits to no great systems of theoretical constructs nor agglomerations of unconscious commands. It is free from both mystical and logical compulsions and — like modern philosophy — is empirical in its attitude to all that comes. (. . .)
> On the more technical side, though of course related to all this, we see refusal to abandon a rational structure and comprehensible language, even when the verse is most highly charged with sensuous or emotional intent.[1]

In contrast to the rational, comprehensible language Conquest applauds here, Hughes's language is a slippery, makeshift, unstable thing; with it Hughes distances himself from the rational voice of the Movement (inherited from liberal humanism) to delineate a self split between a centripetal contract of linguistic, social and cultural norms and taboos and the centrifugal pull of pre-linguistic, unconscious drives inherited from the infant's world of maternal dependency. Hughes's poetry attempts to make concrete these material conditions (unconscious, linguistic, cultural) that structure and determine the way we perceive the world; the self here is less an autonomous, 'metaphysical' (in the sense of existing outside these conditions) entity capable of recognizing and representing the world for what it is (the humanist ideal), than an effect of certain deep-seated ways of perceiving and representing. The empiricism of the Movement poets is imploded in Hughes: given that the self is subject to socially and culturally specific ways of seeing and speaking, as well as to asocial drives of which it is not conscious, its knowledge of reality as such must be thrown into doubt (or so Hughes seems to imply). Hughes's poetry — its playful anthropomorphism — increasingly comes to suggest the illusory nature of everyday reality by insinuating the role that consciousness itself plays in shaping the phenomenal world.

Seamus Heaney sums up the literary and cultural significance of the Hughes voice as it first made itself heard:

> Hughes's voice, I think, is in rebellion against a certain kind of demeaned, mannerly voice. It's a voice that has no truck with irony because his dialect is not like that . . . I mean, the voice of a generation — the Larkin voice, the Movement voice, even the Eliot voice, the Auden voice — the manners of that speech, the original voices behind that poetic voice, are those of literate English middle-class culture, and I think Hughes's great cry and call and bawl is that English language and English poetry is longer and deeper and rougher than that. That's of a piece with his interest in Middle English, the dialect, his insisting upon foxes and bulls and violence. It's a form of calling out for more, that life is more. And of course he gets back from that middle-class school the enmity he implicitly offers.[2]

In drawing on the energies of dialect (Hughes grew up in West and South Yorkshire), Hughes's poems not only constitute a 'rebellion' against the dominant poetic temperament of the time, they also seek to make felt the social and cultural (even regional) context of their own production. If Hughes's poems attempt to 'call out for more', in Heaney's words, they do so with their hands loaded down with the contingencies of language and culture.

THE EAST EUROPEAN INFLUENCE

Finding no allies in the Movement, with *Wodwo* (1967) and *Crow* (1970, 1972) in particular Hughes begins to draw on the example of East European poetry (Vasko Popa, Miroslav Holub, Zbigniew Herbert, János Pilinszky), a poetry born out of the experience of the second world war, the concentration camps and post-war totalitarianism which adopts a tentative and distrustful stance towards what can be said to be 'real', as well as what the self can be said to be. As Hughes writes of Vasko Popa:

His poems are trying to find out what does exist, and what the conditions really are. The movement of his verse is part of his method of investigating something fearfully apprehended, fearfully discovered. (. . .)

The air of trial and error exploration, of an improvised language, the attempt to get near something for which he is almost having to invent the words in a total disregard for poetry or the normal conventions of discourse, goes with his habit of working in cycles of poems. He will trust no phrase with his meaning for more than six or seven words at a time before he corrects his tack with another phrase from a different direction. In the same way, he will trust no poem with his meaning for more than fifteen or so lines, before he tries again from a totally different direction with another poem.[3]

Hughes might be describing his own method here, the way in which the poems are borne along by a kind of linguistic restlessness that seems rooted in a deep distrust of language, as if the real thing here were somehow beyond language. In effect Hughes looks towards Eastern Europe in *Wodwo* and *Crow* for a linguistic or poetic methodology, a way of approaching through language what is finally unspeakable. Hughes writes:

The silence of artistic integrity 'after Auschwitz' is a real thing. The mass of the human evidence of the camps, and of similar situations since, has raised the price of 'truth' and 'reality' and 'understanding' beyond what common words seem able to pay. The European poets who have been formed by this circumstance are well known. They have only continued to write, when at all, with a seasoned despair, a minimal, much-examined hope, a special irony.[4]

The 'special irony' of Hughes's language is precisely its implicit awareness of its arbitrary and makeshift relation to 'truth' or 'reality': to take this language at face value is to miss not only the ironic inflection, but the poetry itself.

HUGHES AND MYTH

Hughes draws on myth in a way that bears out on another level the implications of his 'improvised' language. His major work of non-fiction, *Shakespeare and the Goddess of Complete Being* (1992), is a massive and intricate reading of Shakespeare in terms of myth. While the title seems unequivocally to give myth the last word, Hughes is careful to point up his reading of myth as an improvised symbol system or language for un-conscious contents. For Hughes any symbol system — mythological or psychoanalytical — that presumes to get a hold on the unconscious can only be provisional and displaced in relation to it; Hughes's mapping of what he calls Shakespeare's 'Tragic Equation' (a compound of myths) carries with it a sense of its own status as a makeshift 'metaphor' for something 'psychological' (and in the final analysis 'incomprehensible'):

> The myths I trace are, as I have indicated, basically only two branches of a single stem, plus another myth that embraces both branches in a crowning unit.
>   If it could be regarded as a mythical 'picture' of the interplay of the right lobe of the brain and the left lobe, and that single stem as the brain stem, one would need no further learning to grasp the real life of the Tragic Equation or its minute-by-minute activity within one's own mind. Or if they can be seen as dramatizations of the phases through which the human male grows up, the psychological stages from dependent infancy to rebelliously independent adolescence, and thereafter to mature resolution of those two antithetical periods of feeling, in a realistic synthesis of all the (finally incomprehensible) exigencies of being briefly alive, then again, the myths will appear simply as a metaphorical language for the job.[5]

In the end, Hughes's use of myth as a means of making sense of what is 'finally incomprehensible' in the self implicitly suggests the inherent provisionality of all human meaning, whether primitive-mythical or rational-scientific (Hughes's ever-readiness to use the language of science as well as of myth in his poems is typical of the kind of discursive cross-breeding that marks his work, and suggests an impatience with any single, self-contained, 'authoritative' code of meaning). In other words, Hughes's use of myth reflects not only the poet's interest in anthropology, religion and psychology, but also something inherent in the very language of the poems: Hughes's language is first and foremost a makeshift language, the poems make no bones about their provisional status in attempting to reclaim (albeit self-consciously) some kind of workable human meaning from a universe fast being evacuated of human meaning by the technocratic bias of modern life.

More precisely, Hughes uses myth in the full knowledge that he is tackling the same psychical space and mechanisms that psychoanalysis 'translates' within its own terms. In an essay on T. S. Eliot Hughes writes:

> We have no problem nowadays in seeing that the God-centred metaphysical universe of the religions suffered not so much an evaporation as a translocation. It was interiorized. And translated. We live in the translation, where what had been religious and centred on God is psychological and centred on an idea of the self — albeit a self that remains a measureless if not infinite question mark. (. . .)
>   In the end, of course, nothing disrupted the basic arrangements. The translation was first class. An ordinary ego still has to sleep and wake

with some other more or less articulate personality hidden inside it, or behind it or beneath it, who carries on, just as before, living its own outlandish life, and who turns out, in fact, to be very like the old poetic self: secularized, privatized, maybe only rarely poetic, but recognizably the same, autonomous, mostly incommunicado, keeper of the dreams. Psychoanalysis simply re-drafted the co-tenancy contract in the new language.[6]

Where Hughes approaches the insights of psychoanalysis through myth, this book looks to translate the other way: what I wanted was as clear an X-ray as possible of how Hughes's language works, and of the implications for the self and its grasp of reality that can be drawn from this practice. It seemed to me that only a theoretical reading of the poems could develop this without leaving the picture cloudy.

In this light a post-structuralist reading is particularly appropriate to Hughes. The theories of Jacques Lacan, especially the 'misrecognition' of the 'Real'[7] that Lacan ascribes to the ego — a misrecognition bound up with the self's subjection to a culturally imposed language and identity — and Julia Kristeva, who sees poetic language as representing a risky practice for rational consciousness in so far as it delves into the constitutive processes and repressions on which such consciousness is founded, are particularly useful in providing an interpretative context that can account for the assault on received notions of self and reality to be found in Hughes. The language theories of Mikhail Bakhtin and Roland Barthes will also be used to shed light on the increasingly complex textual strategies Hughes improvises to this end. Rather than attempt to outline the often dense theories of Lacan, Kristeva and Bakhtin here, I have tried to introduce various aspects piecemeal at points at which they seemed most relevant; for example, Lacan's concept of the 'mirror stage' in child development is outlined in relation to *Crow* (Chapter two), while Kristeva's theory of the 'semiotic *chora*' that manifests itself in poetic language is explained in relation to *Cave Birds* (Chapter four). The idea is that the theoretical context will be picked up more easily along the way.

HUGHES AND SHAMANISM

Linked to Hughes's use of myth is the poet's interest in shamanism. According to Hughes:

Shamanism is not a religion, but a technique for moving in a state of ecstasy among the various spiritual realms, and for generally dealing with souls and spirits, in a practical way, in some practical crisis. It flourishes alongside and within the prevailing religion. (. . .) And whereas religions may differ fundamentally, the inner experiences and techniques and application of Shamanism spring into shape everywhere similarly, as if the whole activity were something closer to biological inevitability than to any merely cultural tradition — though obviously cultural traditions influence it a good deal too, in detail.[8]

A problem is posed for the critic at the point at which Hughes proposes an analogy between shamanism and poetry (and by implication his own poetry):

(. . .) the initiation dreams, the general schema of the shamanic flight, and the figures and adventures they encounter, are not a shaman monopoly: they are, in fact, the basic experience of the poetic temperament we call 'romantic'. In a shamanizing society, *Venus and Adonis*, some of Keats's longer poems, *The Wanderings of Oisin*, *Ash Wednesday*, would all qualify their authors for the magic drum; (. . .) The shamans seem to undergo, at will and at phenomenal intensity, and with practical results, one of the main regenerating dramas of the human psyche: the fundamental poetic event.[9]

From Hughes's description, exactly what this 'fundamental poetic event' entails remains unclear. On a thematic level, interpretative analogies can be drawn between the usual shamanistic motifs of flight/ descent/ dismemberment/ death/ return and certain recurrent motifs and paradigms in Hughes's poetry[10] (this seems to be the basis of Hughes's own identification of the 'romantic' poet with the shaman). Yet such a reading fails to tackle the question of how, if at all, the *language* of the poet may be designated as functioning in a 'shamanistic' way.

To take up this question it is necessary to establish a theoretical context in which Hughes's conflation of shaman and poet can be placed. Given the sheer remoteness in time and space of the primitive shaman from the contemporary Western poet, the structural methodology of Lévi-Strauss seems appropriate. Lévi-Strauss writes: 'If, as we believe to be the case, the unconscious activity of the mind consists in imposing forms upon content, and if these forms are fundamentally the same for all minds — ancient and modern, primitive and civilized (as the study of the symbolic function, expressed in language, so strikingly indicates) — it is necessary and sufficient to grasp the unconscious structure underlying each institution and each custom, in order to obtain a principle of interpretation valid for other institutions and other customs, provided of course that the analysis is carried far enough'[11]. Both primitive shaman and contemporary poet are simultaneously products of and manipulators of a system of representations (i.e. a culture), and it is on this structural plane that analogies between the practices of each may be legitimately pursued.

Lacan follows Lévi-Strauss in finding the speaking being subject to a pre-existing system of language, a network of signs that supports a given culture. Lacan calls this network the Symbolic order. Within this network words are meaningful only in relation to other words; language here has no direct purchase on anything 'real'. Lacan writes:

> (. . .) language cannot be conceived of as the result of a series of shoots, of buds, coming out of each thing. The name is not like the little asparagus tip emerging from the thing. One can only think of language as a network, a net over the entirety of things, over the totality of the real. It inscribes on the plane of the real this other plane, which we here call the plane of the symbolic.[12]

By placing the phenomenon of shamanism within the context of Lacan's and Lévi-Strauss's theory of the Symbolic, the question can be asked as to how far a contemporary poet, working with and within a modern Symbolic order, can be said, in Hughes's own words, 'to qualify for the magic drum'.

Mircea Eliade's commentary on the relationship between shamanism and the cosmology of the tribe is suggestive of certain elementary Symbolic functions on the shaman's part. What is immediately noticeable about the examples of cosmological systems Eliade gives is their homespun quality:

> The Turko-Tatars, like a number of other peoples, imagine the sky as a tent; the Milky Way is the 'seam'; the stars, the 'holes' for light. According to the Yakut, the stars are the 'windows of the world'; (. . .) The sky is also conceived as a lid; sometimes it is not perfectly fitted to the edges of the earth, and then the great winds blow in through the crack. It is likewise through this narrow crack that heroes and other privileged beings can squirm to enter the sky.[13]

The 'great winds' that 'blow in through the crack' in the cosmological system suggest the daunting nature of what falls beyond this system. This extra-Symbolic residue can be usefully designated as the Lacanian 'Real': the Real for Lacan is what is 'impossible' for the human mind, in so far as it falls beyond the network of language through which we make sense of the world. It is what language covers over and what 'resists symbolisation absolutely'[14], and is characterized by Lacan by terms such as 'ineffable', 'unassimilable' and 'intractable'. Eliade's own use of the term 'real' as it relates to the shaman's mystical flight appears to bear similar implications: 'Only for the [shaman] is *real communication* among the three zones a possibility'[15]; that is, the 'reality' of the shamanistic experience consists in the strictest sense in the shaman's ability to effect an ecstatic passage through a postulated rupture in the Symbolic universe ('It is . . . through this narrow crack that heroes and other privileged beings can squirm to enter the sky'), a passage which situates the shaman in the realm of the gods (Lacan: '*The gods belong to the field of the real*[16]').

Strictly speaking, the shamanistic ascent/descent is along the *axis mundi* (Axis of the World) that occupies a place of central importance in primitive cosmologies. Eliade writes:

> This axis, of course, passes through an 'opening,' a 'hole'; it is through this hole that the gods descend to earth and the dead to the subterranean regions; it is through the same hole that the soul of the shaman in ecstasy can fly up or down in the course of his celestial or infernal journeys (. . .)
>
> The Axis of the World has been concretely represented, either by the pillars that support the house, or in the form of isolated stakes, called 'World Pillars.' For the Eskimo, for example, the Pillar of the Sky is identical with the pole at the center of their dwellings. The Tatars of the Altai, the Buryat, and the Soyot assimilate the tent pole to the Sky Pillar.[17]

The imagery of Hughes's poem 'Wind', from *The Hawk in the Rain*, seems to belong to a similar sort of cosmology to those Eliade describes:

> At noon I scaled along the house-side as far as
> The coal-house door. I dared once to look up —
> Through the brunt wind that dented the balls of my eyes
> The tent of the hills drummed and strained its guyrope,
>
> The fields quivering, the skyline a grimace,
> At any second to bang and vanish with a flap:

The wind signified here, which threatens to tear through and blow away the fabric of I-speaker's world (house, hills, fields, skyline), recalls the 'great wind' that blows in through the 'crack' in primitive cosmologies. The I-speaker is reluctant to budge from the sheltering centrality of the house-side, a kind of *axis mundi* around which the poem's images and metaphors are oriented: in this the poem's speaker displays the kind of resistance to 'opening negotiations with whatever happened to be out there' that Hughes identifies in the post-war poetry of the Movement:

> One of the things those poets had in common I think was the post-war mood of having had enough . . . enough rhetoric, enough overweening push of any kind, enough of the dark gods, enough of the id, enough of the Angelic powers and the heroic efforts to make new worlds. (. . .) The second world war after all was a colossal negative revelation. (. . .) it set them dead against negotiation with anything outside the cosiest arrangement of society. They wanted it cosy. (. . .) They were like eskimos in their igloo, with a difference. They'd had enough sleeping out. Now I came a bit later. I hadn't had enough. I was all for opening negotiations with whatever happened to be out there.[18]

Hughes's point seems to be that the provincialism and empiricism of the Movement spring from a Symbolic order as limited and provisional in its relationship to whatever falls outside itself as anything to be found in primitive Symbolic orders: 'At any second to bang and vanish with a flap'. In listening to and opening itself to other tongues (Hughes's interest in religion, myth and anthropology), Hughes's poetry militates against what he sees as the 'cosy' parochialism of the Movement to broach a space where all human meaning begins to appear naked and provisional.

Later poems of Hughes's such as 'Widdop', from *Remains of Elmet* (1979), tend to figure and enact this 'shamanistic' movement through and beyond the Symbolic network. The poem's simple narrative progression outlines an imagined step-by-step construction of a moorland landscape from a postulated 'nothing', the taut, childish phrasing — 'Trees, holding hands, eyes closed,/ Acted at world' — strengthening the impression that the landscape constitutes its own support, as if holding itself together over a void. In effect the poem implicates the dynamics of consciousness itself in the landscape's phenomenal form. The child-like form (a story) and diction ('Trees, holding hands') are pared down to such an extent that it is as if the lines escaped between bated breath: this bracing quality of the poem suggests not only the bracing Pennine winds, but also a primary desire of human consciousness to invest 'the entirety of things' (Lacan) with a veil of meaning, to hold everything together in a narrative, a desire generated by the spectre of 'nothingness' from which this 'fabric' of meaning materializes and against which it is pitted:

Nothing else
Except when a gull blows through
A rip in the fabric
Out of nothingness into nothingness

In this the poem's anthropomorphism is self-reflective: the landscape of the poem returns to us an image of our participation in its very form ('Trees, holding hands, . . .') while positing an ineffable Real on the far side of this image: the 'wind' that blows in from 'between the stars' again suggests the 'great winds' of primitive cosmologies that blow in through the crack between earth and sky.

It is in this 'concretization' of our linguistic and imaginative implication in our world — the above poem's stark and infantile anthropomorphism insinuating the role played by pre- and unconscious operations in the creation of the phenomenal world — that what is perhaps 'the fundamental event' of much of Hughes's poetry may be located. Undermining though not obliterating its representational aspect, Hughes's language relativizes itself in a context — the beyond of language, the Real — that is theoretically infinite, and within which the relativity of the self's coming-into-being is crystallized. The poems are the trace of this subjective 'flight' as such, improvising a space in which the Real may be made to signify, even if what is always signified in the end are the very limitations of consciousness the poet seeks to extend. In this, Hughes's poetry constitutes a sustained attempt to realize the full potential of subjectivity as a creative and signifying activity — an activity that for Hughes entails the imaginative re-creation of 'the world of things' from a contemporary universe that is in Hughes's words 'completely uninhabited except by atoms and the energy of atoms'.[19]

In two essays entitled 'Myth and Education' (1970 and 1976), Hughes writes of a disabling 'passivity in the face of the facts, this detached, inwardly inert objectivity' that, he argues, 'has become the prevailing mental attitude of our time'[20]; he goes on to stress the importance of what he sees as a neglected faculty today: the imagination:

> The inner world, separated from the outer world, is a place of demons.
> The outer world, separated from the inner world, is a place of
> meaningless objects and machines. The faculty that makes the human
> being out of these two worlds is called divine. That is only a way
> of saying that it is the faculty without which humanity cannot really
> exist. It can be called religious or visionary. More essentially, it is
> imagination which embraces both outer and inner worlds in a
> creative spirit.[21]

In what is perhaps his most difficult book, *Cave Birds* (1978), Hughes sets out a kind of imaginative charting of the 'inner world'. In the Note to his *Selected Poems 1957–1981* (1982), Hughes outlines the book's procedure: 'This is a sequence of twenty-nine poems written to accompany drawings — of imaginary birds — by Leonard Baskin. The poems plot the course of a symbolic drama, concerning disintegration and re-integration, with contrapuntal roles played by birds and humans'. A full discussion of the book's method will be found in Chapter four. It suffices here to note how the shifting use of personal pronouns in and between poems effectively decentres and suspends the traditional expressive intentionality of the lyric 'I' by denying it any final say, giving concrete dialogical impetus to the opening up of normally repressed or languageless areas of experience (the life of the body, dreams, death) in the sequence:

> The disputation went beyond me too quickly.
> When I said: 'Civilisation,'
> He began to chop off his fingers and mourn.
>
> > 'After the first fright'

But she was murmuring: Right from the start, my life
Has been a cold business of mountains and their snow
Of rivers and their mud

'In these fading moments I wanted to say'

You just see he is filling the eyes of your friends
And now lifting your hand you touch at your eyes

Which he has completely filled up
You touch him

You have no idea what has happened
To what is no longer yours

'The executioner'

Eliade's summary remarks on the cultural function of the shaman serve
equally well as a commentary on Hughes's and Baskin's speaking birds:

> The lands that the shaman sees and the personages that he meets during
> his ecstatic journeys in the beyond are minutely described by the shaman
> himself, during or after his trance. The unknown and terrifying world of
> death assumes form, is organized in accordance with particular patterns;
> finally it displays a structure and, in course of time, becomes familiar and
> acceptable. In turn, the supernatural inhabitants of the world of death
> become *visible*; they show a form, display a personality, even a biography.
> (. . .) In the last analysis, the accounts of the shamans' ecstatic journeys
> contribute to 'spiritualizing' the world of the dead, at the same time that
> they enrich it with wondrous forms and figures.[22]

It is precisely this improvised Symbolic form or organization or structure
that Lévi-Strauss credits with facilitating the shamanistic cure:

> The shaman provides the sick woman with a *language*, by means of
> which unexpressed, and otherwise inexpressible, psychic states can be
> immediately expressed. And it is the transition to this verbal expression
> — at the same time making it possible to undergo in an ordered and
> intelligible form a real experience that would otherwise be chaotic and
> inexpressible — which induces the release of the physiological process,
> that is, the reorganization, in a favorable direction, of the process to
> which the sick woman is subjected.[23]

Lévi-Strauss's use of the word 'real' again brings to mind the Lacanian
Real, an archaic formulation of which can, as mentioned, be read in the
'crack' or 'hole' in the given cosmological system: a hole towards which
the practising shaman is strictly oriented. It is in the attempt to express
what is 'otherwise inexpressible' (the Symbolic hole or blind spot), in the
process 'reorganizing' the self, that the 'symbolic drama' of *Cave Birds* in
particular finds its cathartic field. More generally, Hughes writes poems
that embody a repeated attempt to broach a space (the unconscious, 'noth-
ingness', the Real) that precedes and outflanks the self and its language, in

Introduction

order to hold out the possibility of new, if provisional and open-ended, understandings of our place in the world.

NOTES

1. Robert Conquest (ed.), *New Lines: An Anthology* (London: Macmillan, 1956), pp. xiv–xv.
2. John Haffenden, Interview with Seamus Heaney, in Haffenden, *Viewpoints: Poets in Conversation with John Haffenden* (London: Faber, 1981), pp. 73–74.
3. Ted Hughes, *Winter Pollen: Occasional Prose* (London: Faber, 1994), pp. 223, 226.
4. *Ibid.*, p. 232.
5. Ted Hughes, *Shakespeare and the Goddess of Complete Being* (London: Faber, 1992), p. 36.
6. Hughes, *Winter Pollen*, pp. 274–275.
7. In the text I use initial capitals to indicate when the words Real, Imaginary and Symbolic are being used in the Lacanian sense.
8. Hughes, *Winter Pollen*, p. 56.
9. *Ibid.*, p. 58.
10. For examples of this approach see Stuart Hirschberg, *Myth in the Poetry of Ted Hughes* (Dublin: Wolfhound Press, 1981) and Michael Sweeting, 'Hughes and Shamanism', in Keith Sagar (ed.), *The Achievement of Ted Hughes* (Manchester: Manchester University Press, 1983). It is an interesting question as to what extent shamanistic fantasies of dismemberment etc. are explicable in terms of Lacan's theory of a retrospective pull toward fragmentation present in the formation of the ego, a pull manifest in certain psychically charged images Lacan terms '*imagos of the fragmented body*': 'images of castration, mutilation, dismemberment, dislocation, evisceration, devouring, bursting open of the body' (Jacques Lacan, *Écrits: A Selection* trans. Alan Sheridan, London: Tavistock/Routledge, 1977, p. 11). These 'imagos', which Lacan finds realized in the paintings of Hieronymus Bosch, read like an itinerary of the initiatory torments of the shaman and suggest the psychological nexus of such an ordeal. A more detailed discussion of Lacan's theory of the 'fragmented body' is to be found in chapter two in relation to *Crow*.
11. Claude Lévi-Strauss, *Structural Anthropology* trans. Claire Jacobson and Brooke Grundfest Schoepf (London: Penguin, 1963), p. 21.
12. Jacques Lacan, *The Seminar of Jacques Lacan Book 1. Freud's Papers on Technique 1953–1954* ed. Jacques-Alain Miller, trans. John Forrester (Cambridge: Cambridge University Press, 1988), p. 262.
13. Mircea Eliade, *Shamanism: Archaic Techniques of Ecstasy* trans. Willard R. Trask (London: Routledge, 1964), p. 260.
14. Lacan, *The Seminar of Jacques Lacan Book 1*, p. 66.
15. Eliade, p. 265.
16. Jacques Lacan, *The Four Fundamental Concepts of Psychoanalysis* ed. Jacques-Alain Miller, trans. Alan Sheridan (London: Penguin, 1977), p. 45.

13

17. Eliade, pp. 259, 261.
18. Ekbert Faas, 'Ted Hughes and *Crow*', Interview with Ted Hughes, *London Magazine* vol. 10 no. 10, January 1971, pp. 10–11.
19. Ted Hughes, 'Myth and Education', in *Children's Literature in Education* 1, 1970, p. 63.
20. *Ibid.*, p. 56.
21. Hughes, *Winter Pollen*, p. 151.
22. Eliade, pp. 509–510.
23. Lévi-Strauss, p. 198.

CHAPTER ONE
Early Hughes

'ARCHAIC ENERGIES'

The title poem which opens Hughes's first volume of poems, *The Hawk in the Rain* (1957), places its speaker in a landscape of violent experience and hallucination:

> I drown in the drumming ploughland, I drag up
> Heel after heel from the swallowing of the earth's mouth,
> From clay that clutches my each step to the ankle
> With the habit of the dogged grave, but the hawk
>
> Effortlessly at height hangs his still eye.
> His wings hold all creation in a weightless quiet,
> Steady as a hallucination in the streaming air.

The pummelling, Middle-English stresses and full vowels of the first stanza threaten to overwhelm the sense of the lines, while the proliferation of fricative consonants over the enjambment on line four and into the second stanza gives this stanza a buoyant, airy feel: the vertiginous switch between contrasting sound patterns registers on a phonological level the split represented in the poem between mental ideal — the hawk seems to represent an ideal of self-possession for floundering I-speaker — and physical reality, as if the elemental onslaught had reactivated a normally repressed infantile experience of bodily uncoordination and helplessness. The homophone I/ eye suggests a dialectic between the I-speaker's experience of turbulent disorder and the *illusion* ('Steady as a hallucination') of transcendence embodied by the hawk, as if the former necessitated and propelled the latter. In this the poem insinuates the delusive mechanics at work behind the 'metaphysical' self, a self that seeks its ideal unity only at the cost of repressing its bodily reality.

The theme of beset selfhood is pursued in various forms in *The Hawk in the Rain*, forming the gist of both the 'love' poems ('Song', 'Parlour-Piece', 'The Dove Breeder', 'Billet-Doux', 'A Modest Proposal', 'Incompatibilities') and war poems ('The Casualty', 'Bayonet Charge', 'Six Young Men'), as well as of the less successful discursive poems — 'Egg-Head' and 'The Man Seeking Experience Enquires His Way of a Drop of Water' — which posit an Olympian perspective on human folly that seems out of key with Hughes's intimation of the illusory status of the unitary, metaphysical self.

The animal poems of the volume — 'The Jaguar', 'The Thought-Fox' and 'The Horses' — are in this sense more successful in that they forestall the possibility of an all-knowing, didactic, 'authoritative' voice, a voice that presides over other poems in the same volume. 'The Jaguar' ends:

> He spins from the bars, but there's no cage to him
> More than to the visionary his cell:
> His stride is wildernesses of freedom:
> The world rolls under the long thrust of his heel.
> Over the cage floor the horizons come.

The poem's speaker here is more mesmerized than knowing; the poem echoes Blake's 'The Tyger' as the big cat is elevated — with the aid of the speaker's awed imagination — to universal proportions. The echo of Blake points up Hughes's neo-Romantic conception of the imagination as a creative and regenerative faculty, although in Hughes's case this conception comes to be increasingly subject to a more modern, post-Freudian sense of the failings of language and of the human capacity for self-delusion. However, the muscular language of the last two lines here — the emphatic stress patterns and heavy assonance — seems to want to become what it describes: the poems at this stage show little recognition of any fault line between signifier (word) and signified (thing, concept), a recognition that is to become central to Hughes's later poetic.

The poem 'Pike', from Hughes's second volume *Lupercal* (1960), elaborates a similar intuition to 'The Jaguar', but with more subtlety and irony. The opening stanza begins with a seemingly objective description of the fish (the repeated 'p's emphasize the feeling of objective precision):

> Pike, three inches long, perfect
> Pike in all parts, green tigering the gold.
> Killers from the egg: the malevolent aged grin.
> They dance on the surface among the flies.

Even here though, the noun-as-verb 'tigering', conspicuous as the only verb within the opening noun-phrase, seems to signal a potential for imaginative disturbance within the factual, specimen-case style of description, while the weirdly enigmatic 'grin' seems to signal that something about the fish remains unaccounted for. The last line of the stanza has a kind of fleeting, anarchic suggestiveness about it: the fish are dancing 'on the *surface*' of the water 'among the flies', defying their empirical confines and anticipating the disorientating perspectives of the final stanza.

The conceit with which the second stanza opens — the pike 'move, stunned by their own grandeur' — registers more overtly the speaker's imaginative participation in the pike's movement. By the last line of this stanza the fish have swollen (much like the jaguar in the earlier poem) from their initial length of 'three inches long' to 'A hundred feet long in their world', while later in the poem the pond (itself enlarged from 'fifty feet across' to become 'as deep as England') is said to hold 'Pike too immense to stir'. The poem's preoccupation with measuring implies a critique of empiricism; the description shifts ground in the poem from objective detail to an apprehension of something primordial that defies and threatens to supplant rational consciousness. The influence of Jung can be felt here — Jung writes: 'We may be able to indicate the limits of consciousness, but the unconscious is simply the unknown psyche and for that reason illimitable because indeterminable. Such being the case, we should not be in the least surprised if the empirical manifestations of unconscious contents bear all the marks of something illimitable, something not determined by space and time. This quality is numinous and therefore alarming, above all to a cautious mind that knows the value of precisely delimited concepts'[1]. This 'illimitable' unconscious remains undefined in Hughes's poem (the poem is about more than a type of fish); it is not caught or 'delimited' but slips the net of numbers and measurements cast by the poem's speaker:

Three we kept behind glass,
Jungled in weed: three inches, four,
And four and a half: fed fry to them —
Suddenly there were two. Finally one

With a sag belly and the grin it was born with.

As the empirical calculations come to nothing within their own inexorable logic, we retain only the image of the mocking, *knowing* grin, a grin which suggests a sardonic appraisal of 'The objective, scientific, fact watching attitude, (. . .) this detached, passively recording attitude' that Hughes insists 'is useless in the most vital activity of all. The activity of understanding ourselves'[2]. The dialectic the poem establishes between this 'detached, passively recording attitude' ('A pond I fished, fifty yards across'), and the stirrings of an awed imagination ('It was as deep as England'), finds its apotheosis towards the end of the poem: the dreamlike subversion of the quotidian world, evocatively captured in the image of the 'Owls hushing the floating woods', with the line's nervous, shuddering assonance, brings with it a concomitant decentring of the rational self, pointed up by the paradox of intentionality contained in 'I dared not cast/ But silently cast' and the confusion of hunter and hunted in the final stanza. The menacingly non-finite 'watching', on which the poem ends, leaves the I-speaker poised on the threshold of a psychical realm whose edges evade fixity, and whose aggressive, primordial phantoms threaten with engulfment the empirical ground upon which the rational self stands.

Stylistically, the poem is saved from portentousness by the way in which, as Leonard Scigaj puts it, 'the tone acts as a buffer against the sensationalism of the most memorable of the details'[3]. Knowledgeable understatement — 'And indeed they spare nobody' — turns to comic overstatement — 'With the hair frozen on my head' — as the speaker's empirical bearings begin to slide and the pike (and what they represent) come into their own. The language of the poem is accordingly more careful and tentative than that of 'The Jaguar' and other early poems — the primordial thing here resists being embodied in human terms.

The emergence of supplanting energies within the self constitutes what is perhaps the central thematic preoccupation of *Lupercal*. The celebrated animals of the volume — the pike, the hawk, the otter, the thrushes, the 'Bull Moses' — typically function as mirrors in which this inner drama is to some degree apprehended. This is not to deny the concentration the poems focus on the animals *as animals*. The first strength of the poems lies in the way they register the intractable presence of the animal, those aspects of its being that remain finally beyond appropriation in human terms. The bull in 'The Bull Moses' is 'too deep in itself to be called to (. . .) nothing of our light/ Found any reflection in him': it is precisely this sharply focused concentration on the material *otherness* of the animals — an otherness that resists the ego's narcissistic tendency to seek its own 'reflection' in things — that suggests a corresponding negotiation of similarly intractable energies in the self. In 'An Otter' the otter is 'neither fish nor beast' — it fails to reciprocate standard notions and definitions of how things are; the implied analogy in these poems between the animal and something slippery and indefinite in the self is here made explicit: 'So the self under the eye lies,/ Attendant and withdrawn.'

In 'View of a Pig' the I-speaker is disturbed by the sight of a dead pig. What keeps the poem moving is the repeated attempt to *frame* the unsettling sight, to give it a meaning and thus assimilate it to consciousness, an attempt that repeatedly falls flat: 'further off' even than death (somehow outweighing even that particular 'meaning' or concept), the dead pig is not 'able to accuse', it has no 'dignity', it is no 'figure of fun', 'Too dead now to pity', and so on. What seems an idle thought — 'How could it be moved?' — is in this sense the key to the poem's own 'meaning' as such:

the dead pig here embodies what is *intractable* (it cannot be 'moved' within or by language) and thus disturbing for a consciousness that constitutes itself through its ability to represent the world to itself.

The poem 'Mayday on Holderness' revolves the main themes of *Lupercal*. The title of the poem draws on a number of associations (just as the poem itself moves largely by association): apart from Mayday's archaic association with pagan fertility festivals and more recent links with International Labour Day, the title also suggests, in the context of the poem, a distress call, a suggestion confirmed by the later reference in the poem to Gallipoli. The distress call as such is by implication that of 'The small piloting consciousness of the bright-eyed objective intelligence' that Hughes credits with having 'steered its body and soul into a hell'[4]. The 'hell' intimated in the poem is that of the self-sufficient, metaphysical 'piloting consciousness' brought to contemplate its own implication in the cycles and processes of nature, history and — given the adjective 'motherly' — its own unconscious, infantile drives:

> This evening, motherly summer moves in the pond.
> I look down into the decomposition of leaves —
> The furnace door whirling with larvae.

The low, full assonance of the opening line, blurring into the fricatives and nasal resonants that constitute the consonantal staple of the line, suggests a kind of (infantile) sub-verbal murmur, suggesting the collapse of the autonomous 'piloting consciousness' that finds its agency within language. As in 'Pike', the reliability of the empirical world is also undercut, its objects and horizons suggestively blurred: 'From Hull's sunset smudge/ Humber is melting eastward'. The absence of the definite article before 'Humber' anticipates the implied questioning of the status of objects *as stable and discrete objects* in the arbitrary nature of the inventory that follows; the river is:

> A loaded single vein, it drains
> The effort of the inert North — Sheffield's ores,
> Bog pools, dregs of toadstools, tributary
> Graves, dunghills, kitchens, hospitals.
> The unkillable North Sea swallows it all.

This questioning of the phenomenal 'fullness' of the object is to form the basis of Hughes's anthropomorphic technique in later poems such as 'Still Life', 'Sugar Loaf' and 'Pibroch'. 'Mayday' reaches its apotheosis by insinuating the historical implications of the primary fantasies of voracious aggression and disintegration it uncovers within the I, fantasies which, the poem seems to suggest, are rooted in repressed infantile experiences of instability and fragmentation (in this the poem recalls 'The Hawk in the Rain'), a suggestion underlined by the poem's predominantly oral and anal imagery:

The North Sea lies soundless. Beneath it
Smoulder the wars: to heart-beats, bomb, bayonet.
'Mother, Mother!' cries the pierced helmet.
Cordite oozings of Gallipoli,

Curded to beastings, broached my palate,

In an interview Hughes speaks of the way in which contemporary Western culture mismanages such energies as are intimated in 'Mayday':

> Religious negotiations had formerly embraced and humanized the archaic energies of instinct and feeling. They had conversed in simple but profound terms with the forces struggling inside people, and had civilized them, or attempted to. Without religion, those powers have become dehumanized. The whole inner world has become elemental, chaotic, continually more primitive and beyond our control. It has become a place of demons. But of course, in so far as we are disconnected anyway from that world, and lack the equipment to pick up its signals, we are not aware of it. All we register is the vast absence, the emptiness, the sterility, the meaninglessness, the loneliness.[5]

Lacan, discussing the role of aggression in the formation of the ego and 'its role in modern neurosis and in the "discontents" of civilization', comes to a similar conclusion: 'What we are faced with (. . .) is the increasing absence of all those saturations of the superego and ego ideal that are realized in all kinds of organic forms in traditional societies, forms that extend from the rituals of everyday intimacy to the periodical festivals in which the community manifests itself. We no longer know them except in their most obviously degraded aspects'[6]. In this light the title of Hughes's poem — its glance towards the archaic festivals behind the 'degraded' holidays of today — appears to constitute an outcry against what Lacan refers to as 'the promotion of the ego' in contemporary Western culture: 'It is clear that the promotion of the ego today culminates, in conformity with the utilitarian conception of man that reinforces it, in an ever more advanced realization of man as individual, that is to say, in an isolation of the soul ever more akin to its original dereliction'[7]. At the risk of simplifying, the 'original dereliction' that Lacan mentions here seems to refer to the infant's realization of its bodily separateness from its mother, a separateness that the child comes to terms with through identifying with others. Following Lacan, contemporary Western culture, in fostering and promoting ideologies of the individual, forestalls or undoes the type of identifications through which the ego might posit itself *in relation* to its world (relations sealed in the rituals and festivities of archaic societies), the cost of which is a pervasive feeling of loneliness and meaninglessness, of 'dereliction'.

However, Hughes at this stage differs from Lacan in his appeal to instinctual or primordial energies in the self that are in the early animal poems implied to lead a life of their own outside culture; for Lacan, such energies or drives are always already invested in the Symbolic order — the order of social law and language that the self is subject to: pronouncements like 'The unconscious is neither primordial nor instinctual; what it knows about the elementary is no more than the elements of the signifier'[8], or, 'The unconscious is structured like a language'[9], provocatively collapse the traditional boundary between nature and culture, between consciousness and the unconscious; what Lacan is saying is that unconscious mechanisms (such as condensation and displacement[10]) are intimately bound up with linguistic mechanisms (such as metaphor and metonymy), that the 'lack' (the infant's experience of insufficiency and separateness) that inaugurates and governs unconscious desire is in principle the same 'lack' to be found at the heart of language (the sign as 'a presence made of absence'[11] — the absent referent/thing). It is a collapse of this order that is evident in Hughes's third volume, *Wodwo* (1967).

LANGUAGE, NARCISSISM AND EMPTINESS

Between Hughes's first two volumes and the appearance of *Wodwo*, something has happened to the primordial 'instincts' that stalked through the earlier books in the form of totem animals; the speaker of the *Wodwo* poems is faced less with an instinctual threat (and implied promise of salvation) from the depths of the unconscious than with an even more disconcerting spectre: *emptiness*:

> You are a wild look — out of an egg
> Laid by your absence.
>
> In the great Emptiness you sit complacent,
> Blackbird in wet snow.
>
> If you could make only one comparison —
> Your condition is miserable, you would give up.
>
> But you, from the start, surrender to total Emptiness,
> Then leave everything to it.
>
> Absence. It is your own
> Absence
>
> Weeps its respite through your accomplished music,
> Wraps its cloak dark about your feeding.
>
> 'Stations'

21

The blackbird here is unaware of the 'Emptiness' that surrounds it: it is the poem's speaker who is able to make comparisons and is 'miserable', as if *language itself* has opened up this 'Absence' at the heart of things. The overtly clichéd, colloquial phrasing here — 'give up', 'from the start', 'leave everything to it' — is in this sense self-reflective, giving an impression of linguistic arbitrariness and hollowness. Lacan suggestively defines the word as 'a presence made of absence', while Julia Kristeva (drawing on Lacan) writes of 'the truth of the signifier as a mourning for an impossible real'[12]. It is something of this 'truth' about language — 'namely its separability, otherness, death' (Kristeva[13]) — that begins to surface in *Wodwo*. The muscular language of poems like 'The Hawk in the Rain' and 'The Jaguar' — a language that seems to want to physically embody what it describes — now seems somehow off the point; 'Stations' implies the gap between sign and referent, or within the sign, between signifier and signified, to be insurmountable, spreading its 'Emptiness' everywhere. It is as if in *The Hawk in the Rain* and (to a lesser extent) *Lupercal*, the poet has overestimated the potential of language to grasp what it is after, but in *Wodwo* begins to hear its Real 'music' ('separability, otherness, death').

The first section of 'Stations' deals explicitly with death:

> For a while
> The stalk of the tulip at the door that had outlived him,
> And his jacket, and his wife, and his last pillow
> Clung to each other.

'Tulip', 'jacket', 'wife', 'pillow' — co-ordinates of the narcissistic ego (they are all '*his*'), reminders of its presence and centrality (here ironically imploded), 'insulation' against the reality of death. Kristeva outlines the process through which the nascent ego comes to terms with feelings of emptiness and separation, feelings that psychoanalysis finds rooted in the infant's realization of its separateness from its mother: 'If narcissism is a defence against the emptiness of separation, then the whole contrivance of imagery, representations, identifications, and projections that accompany it on the way toward strengthening the Ego and the Subject is a means of exorcising that emptiness. Separation is our opportunity to become narcists or narcissistic, at any rate subjects of representation. The emptiness it opens up is nevertheless also the barely covered abyss where our identities, images, and words run the risk of being engulfed'[14]. 'Stations' attempts to push beyond narcissistic 'contrivance' and on into what Lacan calls the Real (Lacan: 'the little we know about the real shows its antinomy to all verisimilitude'[15]). On the far side of the ego's objects — tulip/jacket/wife/pillow — the Real is as exorbitant as it is inaccessible:

I can understand the haggard eyes
Of the old
Dry wrecks
Broken by seas of which they could drink nothing.

'Stations'

Extending the shipwreck conceit (shattered ego) introduced in the first part of the poem ('The lifeboat coffin had shaken to pieces'), Hughes here is trying to get some sort of conceptual handle on what is, strictly speaking, inconceivable, to break through to what Lacan calls 'the revelation of that which is least penetrable in the real, of the real lacking any possible mediation, of the ultimate real, of the essential object which isn't an object any longer, but this something faced with which all words cease and all categories fail, the object of anxiety *par excellence*'[16].

In confronting the materiality of death, 'Stations', like the earlier 'View of a Pig', finally registers only a self-reflective sense of the inadequacy of its own utterance: the flatly clichéd 'I can understand' is doubly ironic, firstly because the Real (following Lacan) is what falls outside the orbit of human understanding, and on a second, more tenuous level, because to understand this would be to understand the impossibility of mediating this insight through language: this is precisely what the tired, clichéd, 'inadequate' phrase seems to suggest.

'Full Moon and Little Frieda', also from *Wodwo*, traces the split between consciousness and the Real to the child's acquisition of language, an acquisition that precipitates a fall from (a retrospectively imagined) primary unity with the world as the child becomes able to differentiate itself through language from its immediate environment. The poem pivots on a child's sudden jubilant recognition of and naming of the moon: '"Moon!" you cry suddenly, "Moon! Moon!"'. 'Moon' is apparently one of the first words learnt by Hughes's and Sylvia Plath's daughter Frieda[17]. The jubilant irruption of the child's voice here is all the more acute in that it seems to cut into and scatter the 'brimming' maternal fullness of the scene (the cows are 'A dark river of blood, many boulders,/ Balancing unspilled milk'). The child's sudden, exclamatory word in effect *differentiates* something — 'The moon has stepped back' — from the predominant impression of fluid indifferentiation given by the description of the cows, by the same token opening up a gulf across which the child 'points' (signifies). Kristeva writes that 'the *emptiness* that is intrinsic to the beginnings of the symbolic function appears as the first separation between what is not yet an *Ego* and what is not yet an *object*'[18]. According to Kristeva, this 'emptiness' opened up by the child's accession to language and selfhood is 'protected' by narcissism:

'Narcissism protects emptiness, causes it to exist, and thus, as lining of that emptiness, insures an elementary separation. Without that solidarity between emptiness and narcissism, chaos would sweep away any possibility of distinction, trace, and symbolization, which would in turn confuse the limits of the body, words, the real, and the symbolic. The child (. . .) signifies itself as child (. . .) precisely in that zone where *emptiness and narcissism*, the one upholding the other, constitute the zero degree of imagination'[19]. Mirrorlike, the moon of the above poem seems to return the child's gaze, effectively 'lining' the gulf opened up by the child's word with a narcissistic reflection. The description of the moon as an 'artist gazing amazed at a work' seems to imply precisely what Kristeva says: that this moment in child development constitutes the 'zero degree of imagination', the empty space where narcissistic imagination will construct its works.

Although the dominant note of the poem is one of wonder and jubilation, the image of the 'spider's web' and the word 'tempt', with its slight echo of the biblical fall, strike darker, if more fleeting notes. These notes are not pursued in the poem: if anything, the web 'tense for the dew's touch' is evasive — the web is of course set for the fly — as if the speaker did not want to let these more troublesome associations impinge too heavily on the magic of the moment. Yet they are latent. In a sense the 'fall' is the fall of the child into the web or network of signs, into a consciousness supported by lack or emptiness. In this respect 'Full Moon and Little Frieda' is fully of a piece with a poem as seemingly different in tone and focus as 'Stations'; the poems bring into focus the near and far side of narcissism respectively, two sides of the same coin.

Hughes's distinctive use of anthropomorphic imagery in poems such as 'Still Life', 'Sugar Loaf', 'Mountains' and 'Pibroch' (all from *Wodwo*) is structured around the same subjective pole: narcissism/lack. Lacan epigrammatically formulates the Real as 'the lack of the lack'[20]; it is full, without fissure (the fissure levered open in things by language). The 'Outcrop stone' of 'Still Life' '*pretends* to be dead of lack' (my italics), as if in trying to conceive of the stone's material fullness the poem's speaker has inadvertently projected his own (unconscious) feelings of lack and emptiness onto it: 'Hoarding its nothings . . . Even its grimace is empty'. In this way the stone becomes a kind of touchstone for consciousness itself, a self-reflective move pointed up by the overt use of financial jargon in the poem: the stone is 'miserly', 'It thinks it pays no rent', 'As if receiving interest'. Hughes here is playing on the idea of material security as compensation for the 'lack' at the heart of the self (following psychoanalytical theory, the infant 'lacks' the attention of the absent mother, a lack that facilitates its entry into language as a means of representing and adjusting to, but never closing, this lack). The poem in effect addresses the fullness of the material world (the outcrop stone) in order to expose on the rebound the unconscious lack that supports the desire for material wealth (in its inert, unknowable materiality, the stone is in the final analysis impermeable to the intercessions of language — financial or otherwise). The twist at the end of the poem redoubles the irony: in the face of the power of 'The maker of the sea', as fleetingly manifested in a harebell of which the stone is 'ignorant', even the stone's material fullness begins to appear uncertain. This intimation of the stone's ephemerality throws into ironic relief the themes of self-possession and material possession which the poem explores.

'Pibroch' works in much the same way. Here the sea's 'meaningless voice', its indifference to 'its dead and its living', again suggests the Lacanian Real. As with the 'Outcrop stone' of 'Still Life', the landscape here functions as a kind of touchstone or projection screen for the speaker's anthropomorphic conceits, so that in effect it is the speaker's own unconscious contents that are materialized: the sea is 'Probably bored', it suffers from insomnia — these characteristics reflect the state of mind of the poem's speaker; yet given the speaker recognizes the sea is 'without self-deception', the poem is self-conscious in its use of projection. In this respect the pebble in the poem is 'imprisoned' not so much in its own purposeless materiality, but more in the psychic economy of the poem's speaker: as in 'Still Life', it is human consciousness, that is, a consciousness that is linguistically and culturally determined (the Western 'bright-eyed objective intelligence'), that finds static, self-contained objects in nature, objects whose status is rendered questionable when attention is drawn to the point of view they are perceived from. This is the crux of the poem's irony: the poem's speaker recognizes that the stone falls outside human consciousness — 'Created for black sleep' — yet can only imagine its materiality by bringing it *within* the world of consciousness, by conceiving of it as being '*Conscious* of the sun's red spot occasionally/ Then dreaming it is the foetus of God' (my italics). Hughes is pushing at the limits of consciousness here, at the threshold of a Real that gives birth to notions of God as both Symbolic marker and narcissistic insulation (this is perhaps what Lacan means when he writes: 'The gods belong to the field of the real'[21]):

> Minute after minute, aeon after aeon,
> Nothing lets up or develops.
> And this is neither a bad variant nor a tryout.
> This is where the staring angels go through.
> This is where all the stars bow down.
>
> 'Pibroch'

Economic and scientific terminologies — 'Nothing *lets up* or *develops*./ And this is neither a *bad variant* nor a *tryout*' — are out of place here: it is as if invisible quotation marks have congealed about the words. The demonstrative 'This' is repeated as if for support, keeping the poem from foundering in a space — the beyond of linguistic consciousness — where words can achieve no purchase. 'This' is the Real which religion and mysticism ('angels' and 'stars') formerly embraced and now, after the collapse of religion in a scientific age, looms as an emptiness or meaninglessness ('Nothing') that the poet negotiates with the terms available, terms which in the process begin to look increasingly contingent (socially and culturally specific).

'A UTILITY GENERAL-PURPOSE STYLE'

Implicit everywhere in *Wodwo* is the feeling of subjective limitation, that the human subject, tied to a socially and culturally specific language and way of seeing, is incapable of knowing anything outside its terms. Yet these limitations if anything provide the impetus for the poems: uninterested in silence as an alternative, the *Wodwo* poems clamour after a Real they know they can only provisionally represent.

The poem 'Second Glance at a Jaguar', also from *Wodwo*, implies a corrective to the earlier jaguar poem in *The Hawk in the Rain*. In the earlier poem the jaguar is *given* as signified, that is, the signifier 'jaguar' is felt to be enough to establish the point of reference (the signified) from which the speaker's imaginative 'vision' proceeds. However, in the later poem it is as if no amount of signifiers can account for the beast, who is variously described as '*Like* a cat going along under thrown stones ... *Like* a thick Aztec disemboweller ... his head *like* a brazier of spilling embers ... his belly *like* a butterfly' (my italics), and so on. Lacan writes of 'an incessant sliding of the signified under the signifier'[22]; Hughes describes the various possible signifieds the signifier 'jaguar' opens onto: 'he is a beautiful, powerful nature spirit, he is a homicidal maniac, he is a supercharged piece of cosmic machinery, he is a symbol of man's baser nature shoved down into the id and growing cannibal murderous with deprivation, he is an ancient symbol of Dionysius since he is a leopard raised to the ninth power, he is a precise historical symbol to the bloody-minded Aztecs and so on. Or he is simply a demon ... a lump of ectoplasm. A lump of astral energy'[23]. The heavy reliance on simile in the poem in effect points up the unstable, shifting status of the signifier-signified relationship and the arbitrary relationship of signs to the Real: the animal is finally described as being 'soundless', it slides under the poem's repeated attempt to encapsulate it in a simile, being embodied less by any word or conceit than by the pulsating rhythm of the lines.

Hughes here is improvising a language that is open-ended and flexible, aware of its 'displaced' status with regard to what it refers to, yet ready nonetheless to (self-consciously) tackle a Real that resists human thoughts and projections. Hughes's comments on Keith Douglas's language shed light on his own practice: 'It is a language for the whole mind, at its most wakeful, and in all situations. A utility general-purpose style, as, for instance, Shakespeare's was, that combines a colloquial prose readiness with poetic breadth, a ritual intensity and music of an exceedingly high order with clear direct feeling, and yet in the end is nothing but casual speech'[24]. Hughes's language is self-reflective in so far as it always (after *Wodwo*) has one eye on its 'displacement' from the Real, the way it is born of 'nothing but casual speech' — but speech taken to the limit (of what is signifiable).

THE INFLUENCE OF SYLVIA PLATH

Perhaps the most important influence on the style of the *Wodwo* poems is the later poetry of Sylvia Plath, Hughes's estranged wife who committed suicide in 1963. Echoing his descriptions both of Keith Douglas's and Shakespeare's language, Hughes finds Plath's language in the later poems to be finally 'direct, and even plain, speech'[25]. With this language Plath was able, according to Hughes, 'to break down the tyranny, the fixed focus and public persona which descriptive or discoursive poems take as a norm'[26]. Hughes might be describing his own development here, the way the discursive mode of early poems such as 'Egg-Head' and 'The Man Seeking Experience' (both from *The Hawk in the Rain*) gives way to the more casually 'direct' voice of the *Wodwo* poems, as if behind the voice and style of *Wodwo* lay 'the voice that produced *Ariel*'[27].

Yet Hughes's description of Plath's language in the later poems as 'direct' can be misleading. Helen Vendler draws attention to the 'theatrical voice' of later poems such as 'Lady Lazarus': 'Almost every stanza of "Lady Lazarus" picks up a new possibility for this theatrical voice, from mock movie talk ("So, so, Herr Doktor. / So, Herr Enemy") to bureaucratic politeness ("Do not think I underestimate your great concern") to witch warnings ("I rise with my red hair / And I eat men like air"). When an author makes a sort of headcheese of style in this way — a piece of gristle, a piece of meat, a piece of gelatine, a piece of rind — the disbelief in style is countered by a competitive faith in it. Style (as something consistent) is meaningless, but styles (as dizzying provisional skepticisms) are all'[28]. Vendler's description of Plath's 'headcheese of style' — 'a piece of gristle, a piece of meat' etc. — is similar to Hughes's characterization of Shakespeare's language as 'a homely spur-of-the-moment improvisation out of whatever verbal scrap happens to be lying around, which is exactly what real speech is'[29], a description that in turn reflects on Hughes's own 'makeshift' language (from *Wodwo* onward). For Vendler, this 'wanton' aspect of Plath's language has the effect of displacing the focus or centre of the poems: 'Poems like "Daddy" and "Lady Lazarus" are in one sense demonically intelligent, in their wanton play with concepts, myths, and language, and in another and more important sense not intelligent at all, in that they wilfully refuse, for the sake of a cacophony of styles (a tantrum of style), the steady, centripetal effect of thought. Instead, they display a wild dispersal, a centrifugal spin out to further and further reaches of outrage'[30]. Without a centre of gravity, without 'the steady, centripetal effect of thought' to hold them together, these later poems of Plath for Vendler simply spin out of control.

It is also noticeable here how Vendler's 'steady, centripetal effect of thought' echoes Hughes's description of Plath's pre-*Ariel* style — 'the tyranny, the fixed focus (. . .) which descriptive or discursive poems take as a norm' — a fixed/centripetal focus that Plath is (according to Hughes) attempting to break down in her later poems (Hughes locates the pivotal poem in this respect as being 'Poem for a Birthday' [1960]). On Hughes's reading of Plath's poetic development, it is steady, centripetal, linear thought (and its agent — the rational, 'metaphysical' self) that the *Ariel* poems are consciously trying to displace and outstrip. In this light Vendler's objection to Plath's 'tantrum of style' seems off the point: the highly stylized yet unstable voices of a poem like 'Lady Lazarus' are in a sense fully adequate to the dynamic, decentred notion of self they articulate.

'Lady Lazarus' ends: 'Out of the ash/ I rise with my red hair/ And I eat men like air'[31]. That the projected transcendence of self here is couched in one of the most obvious of Hollywood clichés — the sexually voracious red-head — is the poem's final irony: at every turn the voice of these poems finds itself circumscribed, unable to disentangle itself from the voices and discourses and stereotypes it seems to mock. In other words, a poem like 'Lady Lazarus' seems to imply that transcendence (of cultural inscription) is impossible for the speaking being, that no 'essential' self can be posited outside its linguistic and cultural construction: the self here is a kind of cipher, caught up in and deflected along the web of social and cultural discourses in which it finds its identity.

The literary theorist Roland Barthes writes:

How can a text, which consists of language, be outside languages? How *exteriorize* the world's jargons without taking refuge in an ultimate jargon wherein the others would simply be reported, recited? As soon as I name, I am named: caught in the rivalry of names. How can the text 'get itself out' of the war of fictions, of sociolects? — by a gradual labor of extenuation. First, the text liquidates all metalanguage, whereby it is text: no voice (Science, Cause, Institution) is *behind* what it is saying. Next, the text destroys utterly, *to the point of contradiction*, its own discursive category, its sociolinguistic reference (its 'genre'): it is 'the comical that does not make us laugh,' the irony which does not subjugate, the jubilation without soul, without mystique (. . .), quotation without quotation marks. (. . .) It is a matter of effecting, by transmutation (. . .), a new philosophic state of the language-substance; this extraordinary state, this incandescent metal, outside origin and outside communication, then becomes language, and not *a* language, whether disconnected, mimed, mocked.[32]

'Quotation without quotation marks', 'language (. . .) disconnected, mimed, mocked' — Barthes might be describing the reified, jargon-laden language(s) of 'Lady Lazarus' here, much as the speaker of Plath's poem seems to be trying to transcend or 'get out of' her linguistic, social and sexual wrappings in the very manner Barthes describes. There is no single voice or 'metalanguage' behind Plath's poem, no point of stability provided outside the play of discourses through which the self constitutes itself. In so far as everyday speech is never '*a* language' but is born of a kind of loose cross-breeding of many discourses, of various figures of speech, Barthes's notion of 'a new philosophic state of the language-substance' would seem to be at least partially analogous to Hughes's notion of Shakespeare's demotic language: 'a homely spur-of-the-moment improvisation out of whatever verbal scrap happens to be lying around, which is exactly what real speech is'. In other words, Barthes's philosophic 'language-substance' and Hughes's 'utility general-purpose style' perhaps refer to much the same thing, which would at bottom be nothing more than everyday speech, but speech raised to a kind of second power, become self-conscious, self-reflective, relativized (Hughesian 'directness' when it comes to language thus does not preclude self-consciousness).

   In this light, Plath's later poetry constitutes not so much a 'tantrum of style' ('The distress of these poems unbalances them aesthetically' — Vendler[33]), but a highly self-conscious exploration of the intimate relationship between language and identity. As Jacqueline Rose writes in her book on Plath: 'The frequent diagnoses of Plath seem to me to have as at least one of their effects, if not purposes, that they have transposed into a fact of her individual pathology the no less difficult problem of the contradictory, divided and incomplete nature of representation itself'[34]. For Rose, both Plath's and Hughes's poetry is marked by 'the coexistence of complicity and critique', constituting both 'the analysis, and the continuing symptom, of what it describes'[35]. Much as the projected transcendence of self at the end of 'Lady Lazarus' ironically undercuts itself by playing straight into the hands of one of the most obvious cultural stereotypes of the feminine, so Rose finds in Hughes's poem 'Hawk Roosting', from *Lupercal*, a 'simultaneous acting out and the strongest diagnosis' of 'pure identity in its fascist mode'[36]. The poem is a monologue set in the mind of a hawk, but to read the poem as a fairly credible approximation of a hawk's point of view is to fall into the trap the poem sets: this is the illusion the poem simultaneously sustains and punctures — the clipped economy of the sentences and the precise, abstract diction seem to befit a bird of prey, yet at the same time the hawk is thinking in blatantly *human* terms. In this the poem seems to pose the question of how a language and point of view redolent of fascism (the line: 'And the earth's face upward for my inspection' overtly suggests a militaristic point of view) can come to sound 'natural'. Hughes says that when he wrote the poem 'what I had in mind was that in this hawk Nature is thinking', but that the hawk ended up sounding 'like Hitler's familiar spirit'[37]. In this respect the poem, much like Plath's 'Lady Lazarus', seems to constitute an implicit reminder of the impossibility of speaking or thinking without subscribing to the invisible ideologies encoded and 'naturalized' in language.

It is in this sense that Plath's later poetic seems to have left its mark on Hughes's stylistic development: in both the later Plath and the post-*Lupercal* Hughes, the transparency of language — its tendency to 'naturalize' ideological positions — is shattered; in Barthes's words, in this type of writing 'the "natural" begins to stir, to signify (to become once again relative, historical, idiomatic); the (. . .) illusion of the *self-evident* chips, cracks, the machine of language starts up, "Nature" shudders with all the sociality compressed, sleeping, within it'[38]. Or as Hughes says with regard to 'Hawk Roosting': 'It's not so simple maybe because Nature is no longer so simple'[39].

HUGHES AND ROMANTICISM

Thomas West, in his book on Hughes, finds in Hughes's account of Scout Rock, the cliff face that overhangs Hughes's childhood home, a metaphor for the poet's practice: 'In the account of Scout Rock, Hughes by implication assimilates the poet to the rebel, the mountaineer, who counter-attacks the charm of the precipice, sending his thoughts or body over against the oppressive and aggressive limits of the staring natural world. Here poetry, a kind of mountaineering *against* the evil eye of the precipice, is seen as a combative and liberating force'[40]. Certainly Hughes's description of the oppressive presence of the Rock is suggestive of an early and daunting encounter with what is intractable or unassailable for the human mind:

> The most impressive early companion of my childhood was a dark cliff, or what looked like a dark cliff, to the south; a wall of rock and steep woods half-way up the sky, just cleared by the winter sun. This was the *memento mundi* over my birth: my spiritual midwife at the time and my godfather ever since — or one of my godfathers. From my first day, it watched. If it could not see me direct, a towering gloom over my perambulator, it watched me through a species of periscope — infiltrating the very light of my room with its particular shadow.
> From my home near the bottom of the south-facing slope of the valley, that cliff was both the curtain and backdrop to existence. (. . .) you step out of the house, or get off a bus come from elsewhere, and are astounded to see that blackish hogback mass riding directly overhead. Something about the clouds and light, the inclination of the season, or some overnight strengthening of the earth, has reared it right out over you, and you feel to be in the mouth of a vast dripping cave, in some hopeless age. (. . .) Every thought I tried to send beyond the confines of the valley had to step over that high definite hurdle.[41]

Hughes's description in places calls up Wordsworth's boat stealing scene from *The Prelude*. In Wordsworth's poem, the child steals a rowing boat and rows out onto the lake:

> When, from behind that craggy steep (till then
> The bound of the horizon), a huge cliff,
> As if with voluntary power instinct,
> Upreared its head. I struck and struck again,
> And growing still in stature, the huge cliff
> Rose up between me and the stars, and still,
> With measured motion, like a living thing
> Strode after me.[42]

For West, Hughes's Rock differs from Wordsworth's 'huge cliff' 'by the nature of the evil eye that is attributed to it': 'This eye is felt as an inquiring and accusatory presence', this is no 'agent of nature's tutoring spirit'[43]. For this reason, according to West, Hughes's description of the Rock cannot be read 'as some echo of Romantic tradition'[44].

Two things spring to mind here: firstly, Wordsworth's 'huge cliff' is nothing if not an 'inquiring and accusatory presence' for the child, who imagines it pursues him, and after the encounter returns home 'with grave/

And serious thoughts': 'In my thoughts/ There hung a darkness'. On these terms there seems to be little difference between Wordsworth's cliff and Hughes's Rock. Secondly, Hughes's description of Scout Rock seems to consciously echo the episode from Wordsworth's poem — just as the poem 'The Jaguar' recalls Blake's 'The Tyger', or 'Skylarks' (from *Wodwo*) recalls Shelley's 'To a Skylark' — as if in such instances Hughes were self-consciously placing himself within Romantic tradition. Allusions such as these signal Hughes's literary influences and allegiances: the Romantics' reaction against scientific rationality and their concomitant emphasis on the redemptive powers of the imagination directly inform Hughes's vision.

Yet in placing himself in such company Hughes is also drawing attention to his own particular orientation. For instance, Wordsworth's rising cliff is an optical illusion — as the child rows further out onto the lake the cliff appears to loom larger; what is significant here is not so much the material bulk of the cliff as the child's imaginative response to it: the scene seems to figure the birth of the imagination itself, the insistent phallic associations — 'As if with voluntary power instinct,/ Upreared its head . . . growing still in stature . . . Rose up' — connoting its potency and power. For Wordsworth, 'the mind of man' is 'Of substance and of fabric more divine' than 'the earth/ On which he dwells'[45]. Hughes's Rock is of a different order: no trick of the light or imagination, its intractable material presence oppresses the human mind; its effect is like that of a trauma: 'It was not a frightening presence, it was a darkening presence, like an over-evident cemetery. Living beneath it was like living in a house haunted by a disaster that nobody can quite believe ever happened, though it regularly upsets sleep'[46]. This is where Hughes's vision differs from the more idealistic strains of Romanticism: the imagination in Hughes is up against something that resists, limits, oppresses and finally outflanks its power.

Lacan draws on Freud's account of his grandchild's game with a cotton-reel as an exemplary paradigm of the way in which a child comes to master its environment through language. Freud observed how, in the wake of its mother's comings and goings, the child would alternately throw away and retrieve a cotton-reel attached to a string, making sounds similar to the German words for gone — '*fort!*' — and here — '*da!*'. In the spectacle of the child's game with the cotton reel, Lacan sees the passivity of the child in the face of its mother's alternating absence/presence transformed into the playful activity of symbolically representing the perceived absence/presence:

> For the game of the cotton-reel is the subject's answer to what the mother's absence has created on the frontier of his domain — the edge of his cradle — namely, a *ditch*, around which one can only play at jumping.

> This reel is not the mother reduced to a little ball by some magical game worthy of the Jivaros — it is a small part of the subject that detaches itself from him while still remaining his, still retained. This is the place to say, in imitation of Aristotle, that man thinks with his object. It is with his object that the child leaps the frontiers of his domain, transformed into a well, and begins the incantation.[47]

The 'ditch' around which the child symbolically 'jumps' provides the basic paradigm for the child's relationship with the Rock in Hughes's account — 'Every thought I tried to send beyond the confines of the valley had to step over that high definite hurdle' (Hughes's cliff-face is simply Lacan's ditch inverted). The 'object' with which man 'thinks' is the signifier (the cotton reel signifies absence — *'fort'* / presence — *'da'*). Here we have the primary, fundamental pattern not only for the workings of language itself — the word as 'a presence made of absence' (Lacan) — but also, on another level, for Hughes's poetic practice: the way in which the poems, in their linguistic and conceptual 'jumps', perpetually strive to translate experience of the Real into human terms, however provisional these terms prove to be. In effect Hughes's anthropomorphic conceits draw attention to something in the nature of language itself. Hughes writes:

> There are no words to capture the infinite depth of crowiness in the crow's flight. All we can do is use a word as an indicator, or a whole bunch of words as a general directive. But the ominous thing in the crow's flight, the bare–faced, bandit thing, the tattered beggarly gipsy thing, the caressing and shaping yet slightly clumsy gesture of the downstroke, as if the wings were both too heavy and too powerful, and the headlong sort of merriment, the macabre pantomime ghoulishness and the undertaker sleekness — you could go on for a very long time with phrases of that sort and still have completely missed your instant, glimpse knowledge of the world of the crow's wingbeat. And a bookload of such descriptions is immediately rubbish when you look up and see the crow flying.[48]

The gap between word and thing here is insurmountable: the more words, the more the Real thing is 'missed', the more it recedes. Hughes's use of anthropomorphic imagery here accentuates this gap between word and thing; it draws attention to the second-hand, displaced, improvisory qualities of the object — the signifier — with which we think, with which we negotiate our frontiers.

The poem 'Skylarks' recalls Shelley's 'To a Skylark'. Shelley's poem poses the problem of how to conceive of the skylark: 'What thou art we know not;/ What is most like thee?' After a series of similes that attempt to imaginatively evoke its being, the poem's speaker finally posits the bird's flight and song as being irretrievable in human terms:

Better than all measures
  Of delightful sound;
Better than all treasures
  That in books are found —
Thy skill to poet were, thou scorner of the ground![49]

The skylark of Shelley's poem seems to represent an ideal state of poetic inspiration and imaginative flight for the poem's speaker — it is an 'unbodied joy', from which flows 'profuse strains of unpremeditated art'; yet by the same token this state is felt to be unattainable for the poem's earth-bound speaker:

Yet if we could scorn
  Hate and pride and fear;
If we were things born
  Not to shed a tear,
I know not how thy joy we ever should come near.

Hughes's poem follows Shelley's both in its implicit acknowledgement of the inadequacy of human terms and concepts in the face of the skylark's flight, in its recognition of the impossibility of *knowing* the bird, and in its paradoxical attempt to nonetheless try to account for the bird: 'My idleness curdles/ Seeing the lark labour near its cloud' ('Skylarks'); 'Teach me half the gladness/ That thy brain must know' ('To a Skylark') (in this respect Hughes seems closer to Shelley's scepticism — 'What thou art we know not' — than Wordsworth's idealism — 'the mind of man becomes/ A thousand times more beautiful than the earth/ On which he dwells'). Yet Hughes's poem differs from its precursor in shifting emphasis onto the physicality of the lark — Hughes's bird is no 'unbodied joy' but is 'leaden/ With muscle', as though in switching emphasis from the metaphysical to the physical Hughes is checking the more transcendent, idealistic tendencies of Romanticism and relocating the source and nature of ecstatic vision in the body and its drives.

In Hughes's poem, the lark seems to lay down an implicit challenge to the poem's speaker to try to comprehend its flight and song:

My idleness curdles
Seeing the lark labour near its cloud
Scrambling
In a nightmare difficulty
Up through the nothing

Its feathers thrash, its heart must be drumming like a motor,
As if it were too late, too late

Dithering in ether

The 'labour' and 'nightmare difficulty' here are also that of the poem's speaker, who must wrestle with everyday, routine language and concepts

('My idleness curdles') if the Real nature of the lark's flight is to be captured. Hughes here is forcing language and linguistic consciousness 'Up through the nothing', towards that which its terms cannot account for, a sense of which is registered by the anxiously vague 'As if it were too late, too late' and the 'Scrambling' of letters in 'Dithering in ether'. The poem pivots on the impression that an uncrossable threshold has been reached (the disappearance of the signifiable object) — 'the lark is evaporating/ Till my eye's gossamer snaps' — after which the lines lengthen, the rhythm relaxes, 'the sky lies *blank open*' (my italics), suggesting a widened state of consciousness has been reached.

Following Barthes, there is no 'metalanguage' here: while the poem relies heavily on casual speech patterns ('it's a relief', 'they've had enough', 'they're burned out', 'the earth gives them the O.K.'), the language at the same time has — as Hughes writes of Shakespeare's language — 'the air of being invented in a state of crisis, for a terribly urgent job, a homely spur-of-the-moment improvisation out of whatever verbal scrap happens to be lying around, which is exactly what real speech is'. In Barthes's terms, the 'verbal scraps' that make up a poem like 'Skylarks' do not constitute '*a* language', but rather an 'extenuated' state of language, language that, while labouring to represent the skylarks of the poem, continually glances askance at its own arbitrary, makeshift status.

LANGUAGE AND MYSTICISM

The poem 'Gnat-Psalm', also from *Wodwo*, pushes the process further. The muddled consonants of the poem's title suggest a 'scrambling' of language similar to that in 'Skylarks' (language as loose 'scraps': loose turns of phrase and figures of speech). This is picked up thematically in the poem:

When the gnats dance at evening
Scribbling on the air, sparring sparely,
Scrambling their crazy lexicon,
Shuffling their dumb Cabala,
Under leaf shadow

Leaves only leaves
Between them and the broad thrusts of the sun
Leaves muffling the dusty stabs of the late sun
From their frail eyes and crepuscular temperaments
Dancing
Dancing

Writing on the air, rubbing out everything they write
Jerking their letters into knots, into tangles
Everybody everybody else's yoyo

The subject-object distinction produced and upheld by language is here thrown into confusion: 'Everybody everybody else's yoyo'. It is as if the gnats induced a kind of dyslexia in the perceiver — a 'crazy lexicon', the overspill of syllables in 'crepuscular temperaments'. The implicit challenge again here seems to be to find a language adequate to the gnats' transitive being and dance, the spectacle of which outstrips the clumsiness of words. The fluid ephemerality of the gnats is in effect unable to support language — 'Writing on the air, rubbing out everything they write'; the speaker's interpretative moves are simply shaken off: 'Not writing and not fighting but singing'. Kristeva might be describing the poem when she describes the kind of visions of the Real that are not only typical of modernist art, but also of certain forms of psychosis: 'Floating in isolation, this vision of an unnamed real rejects all nomination and any possible narrative. Instead it remains enigmatic, setting the field of speech ablaze only to reduce it to cold ashes, fixing in this way an hallucinatory and untouchable *jouissance*'[50]. 'Gnat-Psalm' ends on an ecstatic apostrophe:

You are the angels of the only heaven!
And God is an Almighty Gnat!
You are the greatest of all the galaxies!
My hands fly in the air, they are follies
My tongue hangs up in the leaves
My thoughts have crept into crannies

Your dancing

Your dancing

Rolls my staring skull slowly away into outer space.

At the limits of the signifiable, to step beyond is to step outside a self supported by language — 'My tongue hangs up in the leaves/ My thoughts have crept into crannies' — and into 'space' (ecstasy: from the Greek *ekstasis* — standing outside oneself).

In foregrounding the limitations and failings of language and linguistic consciousness in this way, Hughes seems to open the door to mysticism, and Hughes's interest in myth and shamanism is in this sense coterminous with his 'utility general-purpose style'. Yet myth or mysticism is never allowed to have last word in the poems: the line 'And God is an Almighty Gnat' in the above poem self-consciously locates the religious/mythical impulse within the same need to *represent* the universe — to make it *meaningful* — that language itself serves. The line suggests the *capriciousness* of (religio-mythic) representation only to celebrate this very capriciousness, as if it were somehow the precondition for creating meaning (the arbitrary relation of the sign to what it refers to makes room for the creative/poetic use of signs). In this light myth begins to appear close to the beginnings of language itself: Hughes seems to imply that all languages are in a sense 'mythical' constructs, provisional attempts to represent the universe within the terms available. As such, myth in Hughes's poetry is subject to the same sense of displacement that marks the very language of the poems: the Real here reverberates through the failings of language and myth, its presence felt but never signified.

NOTES

1. C. G. Jung, *Psychology and Alchemy* second edition, trans. R. F. C. Hull (London: Routledge, 1968), pp. 182–183.
2. Ted Hughes, 'Myth and Education', in *Children's Literature in Education* 1, 1970, p. 57.
3. Leonard M. Scigaj, *The Poetry of Ted Hughes: Form and Imagination* (Iowa: Iowa UP, 1986), p. 71.
4. Ted Hughes, *Winter Pollen: Occasional Prose* ed. William Scammell (London: Faber, 1994), p. 149.
5. *Ibid.*, p. 149.
6. Jacques Lacan, *Écrits: A Selection* trans. Alan Sheridan (London: Tavistock/Routledge, 1977), p. 26.
7. *Ibid.*, p. 27.
8. *Ibid.*, p. 170.
9. Jacques Lacan, *The Four Fundamental Concepts of Psychoanalysis* ed. Jacques-Alain Miller, trans. Alan Sheridan (London: Penguin, 1977), p. 20.
10. Condensation: 'One of the essential modes of the functioning of the unconscious processes: a sole idea represents several associative chains at whose point of intersection it is located'; displacement: 'The fact that an idea's emphasis, interest or intensity is liable to be detached from it and to pass on to other ideas, which were originally of little intensity but which are related to the first idea by a chain of associations'; J. Laplanche and J. -B. Pontalis, *The Language of Psychoanalysis* trans. Donald Nicholson-Smith (London: Karnac, 1988), pp. 82, 121.
11. Lacan, *Écrits*, p. 65.
12. Julia Kristeva, *The Kristeva Reader* ed. Toril Moi (Oxford: Blackwell, 1986), p. 236.
13. *Ibid.*, p. 236.
14. Julia Kristeva, *Tales of Love* trans. Leon S. Roudiez (New York: Columbia University Press, 1987), p. 42.
15. Lacan, *The Four Fundamental Concepts of Psychoanalysis*, p. ix.
16. Jacques Lacan, *The Seminar of Jacques Lacan Book II. The Ego in Freud's Theory and in the Technique of Psychoanalysis 1954–1955* ed. Jacques-Alain Miller, trans. Sylvana Tomaselli (Cambridge: Cambridge University Press, 1988), p. 164.

17. 'Five Poems by Ted Hughes', written and presented by Ted Hughes, for 'The English Programme', Thames Television, 1989.
18. Kristeva, *Tales of Love*, p. 24.
19. *Ibid.*, p. 24.
20. Lacan, *The Four Fundamental Concepts of Psychoanalysis*, p. ix.
21. *Ibid.*, p. 45.
22. Lacan, *Écrits*, p. 154.
23. Ekbert Faas, 'Ted Hughes and *Crow*', Interview with Ted Hughes, *London Magazine* vol. 10, no. 10, Jan. 1971, p. 8.
24. Hughes, *Winter Pollen*, p. 215.
25. Ted Hughes, 'The chronological order of Sylvia Plath's poems', in Charles Newman (ed.), *The Art of Sylvia Plath: A Symposium* (London: Faber, 1970), p. 195.
26. *Ibid.*, p. 191.
27. *Ibid.*, p. 192.
28. Helen Vendler, *The Music of What Happens: Poems, Poets, Critics* (Cambridge, Mass.: Harvard University Press, 1988), p. 282.
29. Hughes, *Winter Pollen*, p. 105.
30. Vendler, p. 282.
31. Sylvia Plath, *Collected Poems* ed. Ted Hughes (London: Faber, 1981), p. 247.
32. Roland Barthes, *The Pleasure of the Text* trans. Richard Miller (Oxford: Blackwell, 1990), pp. 30–31.
33. Vendler, p. 282.
34. Jacqueline Rose, *The Haunting of Sylvia Plath* (London: Virago, 1991), p. 5.
35. *Ibid.*, p. 160.
36. *Ibid.*, pp. 155, 156.
37. Faas, p. 8.
38. Roland Barthes, *Roland Barthes* trans. Richard Howard (London: Papermac, 1995), p. 97.
39. Faas, p. 8.
40. Thomas West, *Ted Hughes* (London: Methuen, 1985), p. 18.
41. Ted Hughes, 'The Rock', in *The Listener* September 19 1963, pp. 421, 422.
42. William Wordsworth, *The Prelude* Book One, lines 406–413, in *Romanticism: An Anthology* ed. Duncan Wu (Oxford: Blackwell, 1994), p. 293.
43. West, pp. 18, 17.
44. *Ibid.*, p. 17.
45. Wordsworth, *The Prelude* Book Thirteen, lines 446–452, in Wu, pp. 473–474.
46. Hughes, 'The Rock', p. 442.
47. Lacan, *The Four Fundamental Concepts of Psychoanalysis*, p. 62.
48. Ted Hughes, *Poetry in the Making: An Anthology of Poems and Programmes from 'Listening and Writing'* (London: Faber, 1967), pp. 119–120.
49. Percy Bysshe Shelley, 'To a Skylark', in Wu, p. 955.
50. Kristeva, *The Kristeva Reader*, p. 227.

CHAPTER TWO

Crow

Two aspects of Hughes's *Crow: From the Life and Songs of the Crow* (1970, 1972) have proved hard to swallow for some critics, namely, the book's language and its imagery, or as Roy Fuller puts it, 'the pathological violence of its language, its anti-human ideas, its sadistic imagery'[1]. Fuller points out three things here, although it might be more accurate to speak of *Crow*'s anti-liberal humanist ideas, assuming that is that *Crow* has any ideas of its own, which is not certain. In any case, the epithet 'anti-human' seems to reflect here only the ideas, or rather ideals, of a certain type of criticism: writing from much the same point of view, Geoffrey Thurley finds *Crow* 'a somewhat inhuman, even brutal book, with none of the broad strength of the best of Hughes's earlier poems. It remains to be seen whether Hughes's abandonment of a human perspective is ultimately justifiable'[2]. The abandonment of a 'human perspective' in *Crow* is really no more than the abandonment of the transparent language of a 'metaphysical' self, a language that bears no recognition of its material (linguistic, cultural, unconscious) determinants. If the book can be conceived of as a reflective surface, then it is a cracked one, one that fails to give any return on humanist preconceptions, or rather returns them in distorted fashion, in pieces. For the critic anticipating the corroboration of certain literary expectations or ideals, *Crow* seems to allow of only one response: in Calvin Bedient's words, 'Hughes is a total nihilist', while *Crow* is 'the croak of nihilism itself'.[3]

CARNIVAL AND TRICKSTER

Other criteria than a 'human[ist] perspective' are clearly needed if *Crow* is to be read as anything more than a nihilistic lack of returns, as a book that sadistically refuses to reciprocate any 'human idea'. Calvin Bedient touches on the crux of the question: 'in most of these poems Hughes wastes himself. A master of language who tosses words on the page — can any aesthetic justify this?'[4]. Given the plurality of discourses that inform *Crow* — biblical narratives, myth, the cartoon-strip, science, psychoanalysis — and bearing in mind the slapstick way in which these discourses are thrown together, the book might be 'justified' after Bakhtin as carnivalesque literature. According to Bakhtin, within the carnivalesque text: 'A free and familiar attitude spreads over everything: over all values, thoughts, phenomena, and things. All things that were once self-enclosed, disunified, distanced from one another by a noncarnivalistic hierarchical worldview are drawn into carnivalistic contacts and combinations. Carnival brings together, unifies, weds, and combines the sacred with the profane, the lofty with the low, the great with the insignificant, the wise with the stupid'.[5]

Hughes himself writes that his 'guiding metaphor' for *Crow* was the figure of the Trickster from primitive tales and mythologies[6]. Paul Radin, in his book on American Indian Trickster mythology, characterizes the Trickster as 'primarily an inchoate being of undetermined proportions, a figure foreshadowing the shape of man'[7]. Similarly, Hughes speaks of Crow's 'ambition to become a man, which he never quite manages'[8]. In effect, Hughes uses the figure of the comic, bungling and irrepressible Trickster in *Crow* as a carnivalesque device; that is, the Trickster grants a licence to improvise, to combine 'the sacred with the profane, the lofty with the low, the wise with the stupid': Crow is as much as anything else the incorrigible prankster of poems like 'A Childish Prank' and 'Crow Blacker than ever', his perverse meddlesomeness affording the poet the means to question and tinker with received theological wisdom. Radin points out that archaic Trickster narratives are to be understood only 'in their specific cultural environments and in their historical settings'[9]. On this reading, Crow as Trickster is a carnivalistic means for conducting an irreverent and raucous critique of contemporary Western culture, and in particular of the combined legacy of Judaeo-Christian morality and scientific rationality (though there is more to *Crow* than cultural critique, as I hope to show).

According to Bakhtin, carnivalesque literature is characterized by 'an indestructible vitality': 'Thus even in our time those genres that have a connection, however remote, with the traditions of the serio-comical preserve in themselves the carnivalistic leaven (ferment), and this sharply distinguishes them from the medium of other genres'.[10] Trying to account for 'the culture gap that seems to render my poem *Crow* nearly inaccessible to some readers', Hughes himself draws a sharp distinction between Trickster literature and the modern tradition of Black Comedy: 'In Black Comedy, the lost hopeful world of the Trickster is mirrored coldly, with a negative accent. In Trickster Literature, the suffering world of Black Comedy, shut off behind thin glass, is mirrored hotly, with a positive accent. It is the difference between two laughters: one, bitter and destructive; the other zestful and creative, attending what seems to be the same calamity'[11]. In an analogous manner, Bakhtin contrasts carnivalesque humour with 'the negative and formal parody of modern times': 'Folk humor denies, but it revives and renews at the same time. Bare negation is completely alien to folk culture'[12]. Tracing carnival forms back to their roots in primitive cultures, Bakhtin comes upon the same mythical prototype which provides Hughes with his 'guiding metaphor' for *Crow*: 'In the folklore of primitive peoples, coupled with the cults which were serious in tone and organization were other, comic cults which laughed and scoffed at the deity ("ritual laughter"); coupled with serious myths were comic and abusive ones; coupled with heroes were their parodies and doublets'[13]. Hughes also relates the figure of the Trickster to 'the infantile, irresponsible naivety of sexual love' — 'At bottom this is what Trickster is: the optimism of the sperm, still struggling joyfully along after 150 million years'[14] — in similar fashion to Bakhtin's linking of carnival forms to bodily life — that which is 'opposed to severance from the material and bodily roots of the world'[15].

In this context — the Trickster as carnivalesque device — the poem 'A Childish Prank' reads like a paradigm of the basic principles of carnivalization. In Bakhtin's words, 'The "absolute past" of gods, demigods and heroes is here (. . .) "contemporized": it is brought low, represented on a plane equal with contemporary life, in an everyday environment, in the low language of contemporaneity'[16]. That Crow's laugh forms the prelude to his crude intervention in theological matters in the poem is significant, suggesting the fundamental role played by laughter in the carnivalizing process. Enigmatic images of laughter, smiling and grinning occur throughout *Crow*, about which Hughes says: 'I'm not quite sure what they signify'[17]. Hughes's comment is perhaps not so disingenuous as it might sound. Laughter as such operates more as a structuring force or principle in *Crow* than as a 'meaning' sufficient to itself; according to Bakhtin, 'Laughter degrades and materializes'[18]:

> It is precisely laughter that destroys the epic, and in general destroys any hierarchical (distancing and valorized) distance. As a distanced image a subject cannot be comical; to be made comical, it must be brought close. Everything that makes us laugh is close at hand, all comical creativity works in a zone of maximal proximity. Laughter has the remarkable power of making an object come up close, of drawing it into a zone of crude contact where one can finger it familiarly on all sides, turn it upside down, inside out, peer at it from above and below, break open its external shell, look into its center, doubt it, take it apart, dismember it, lay it bare and expose it, examine it freely and experiment with it.

> Laughter demolishes fear and piety before an object, before a world, making of it an object of familiar contact and thus clearing the ground for an absolutely free investigation of it.[19]

The comic demolition of 'fear and piety' is integral to the technique of *Crow*. Describing the rapid composition of the poems, Hughes remarks that they 'arrived with a sense of having done something . . . tabu'[20]. Jonathan Raban takes up Hughes's comment, finding in the transgressive qualities of the poems confirmation of their 'essentially social' nature: 'a great deal of their energy, their celebrated "violence", springs from the tension that they tap between the conventionally permitted and the forbidden. Their language, far from being post-Christian, post-civilized, is a language obsessed by institutional rules'[21]. In poems like 'A Childish Prank' Crow functions overtly as a comic device for drawing the 'institutional' object (the biblical Creation myth) 'up close', for 'fingering' it with 'the low language of contemporaneity' (the colloquial directness and slapstick feel of words like 'dragged' and 'stuffed', the pun on 'coming'). As Radin writes of the Trickster's exploits: 'Nothing here has been created *de novo*'[22]; what the poem makes 'new' is achieved by rearranging the old, by meddling with what Hughes identifies as the 'fundamental guiding ideas of our Western civilization (. . .) derive[d] from Reformed Christianity and from Old Testament Puritanism'[23] (in this respect, the comic-serious reinterpretations of the biblical Creation myth in *Wodwo* — 'Reveille' and 'Theology' — obviously anticipate *Crow*).

David Lodge points out the similarities of style and convention that *Crow* shares with the contemporary strip or animated cartoon: 'the caricatured, quasi-human bird reappearing in a series of heterogeneous but familiar contexts; the mixture of comedy and violence; the stark, hard-edged quality of the visual images; the construction of narrative in a series of parallel episodes, or statements, climaxed by some unexpected twist or deflating pay-off line; the sudden transformations, mutations, mutilations, reversals and recoveries, which defy all the laws of logic, physics and good taste; above all, perhaps, the very direct, rapid, economic, simple manner of delivery'[24]. Lodge explains the efficacy of the book's cartoon-like technique: 'The adapted cartoon-style conventionalizes the experience, frames it ironically, puts it at a distance and thus makes it manageable'[25]. Jung's commentary on the function of the Trickster tale in primitive cultures appears to substantiate Lodge's interpretation: 'the story of the trickster is not in the least disagreeable to the Winnebago consciousness or incompatible with it, but, on the contrary, pleasurable and therefore not conducive to repression. It looks, therefore, as if the myth were actively sustained and fostered by consciousness'[26]. Hughes himself writes of 'the basis of Freud's whole therapeutic technique that the right fantasy can free the neurotic, temporarily at least, from his neurosis', that the 'devil of suppressed life stops making trouble the moment he is acknowledged, the moment he is welcomed into conscious life and given some shape where he can play out his energy in an active part of the personality'[27]. Together these comments suggest not only the psychological nexus of the figure of Crow, but also something of the urgency of his role. In an afterword to the same essay ('Myth and Education' [1970]), Hughes speaks of American comics consisting 'to an amazing extent of traditional mythological themes in modern form — Batman and the rest of it — very old recurrent mythological themes for societies in some extreme condition'.[28]

Lodge's analogy certainly holds, yet it is also noticeable how the poems continually point up the limitations and shortcomings of their cartoon-like form. For example, the 'O it was painful' of 'A Childish Prank', on one level a crude joke, nevertheless manages to suggest through the void of the 'O' a primordial experience of pain and lack not configurable in the poem's slapstick language and imagery; similarly, the overtly cartoon-like 'BANG!' of 'Truth Kills Everybody' suggests in its very flippancy the way in which popular culture accommodates and 'conventionalizes' the threat of nuclear war, defusing its reality. Hughes's adoption of the cartoon form in *Crow* is more self-conscious and problematic than Lodge perhaps allows for. These are poems about a technocratic society that Hughes diagnoses as being in an 'extreme condition': the modern cartoon as taken on board in *Crow* is in this light more symptom than therapeutic model. As such the cartoon form does not so much 'frame' the poems (and not all the poems are cartoon-like) as constitute one among the many discursive strata — biblical, scientific, mythical — with which the poems are shot through.

Hughes's characterization of Vasko Popa's 'folklore surrealism' (not to be confused with 'literary surrealism', which for Hughes betokens a demoralized surrender 'to the arbitrary imagery of the dream flow') perhaps best accounts for the carnivalistic and cartoon-like aspects of *Crow* (Popa's poetry is another influence on the style and technique of *Crow*): 'Folklore surrealism (. . .) is always urgently connected with the business of trying to manage practical difficulties so great that they have forced the sufferer temporarily out of the dimension of coherent reality into that depth of imagination where understanding has its roots and stores its X-rays (. . .) In the world of metamorphoses and flights the problems are dismantled and solved, and the solution is always a practical one. This type of surrealism, if it can be called surrealism at all, goes naturally with a down-to-earth, alert tone of free inquiry'[29]. Crow's attempts to alter the terms of the various narratives he finds himself within are both crude and practical: in a number of poems where the theological or existential stakes are high — 'Lineage', 'That Moment', 'Crow Tyrannosaurus', 'A Horrible Religious

Error', 'Crow's Song of Himself' — Crow is primarily concerned with finding something to eat. Against the crudely down-to-earth, 'back to basics' perspectives Crow provides, the cultural and religious codes and assumptions that constitute 'coherent reality' begin to lose their familiar, taken for granted quality, and in the process begin to look 'surreal'.

THE 'DIALOGIC' WORD

What Bakhtin calls 'the direct authorial word'[30] is difficult to locate in *Crow*; in Bakhtin's words, the poet here is speaking '*through* language, a language that has somehow more or less materialized, become objectivized, that he merely ventriloquates'[31]. To employ one of Bakhtin's key terms, the language of *Crow* is to varying degrees 'dialogized' — Bakhtin writes: 'Every type of intentional stylistic hybrid is more or less dialogized. This means that the languages that are crossed in it relate to each other as do rejoinders in a dialogue; there is an argument between languages, an argument between styles of language. But it is not a dialogue in the narrative sense, nor in the abstract sense; rather it is a dialogue between points of view, each with its own concrete language that cannot be translated into the other'[32]. This does not necessarily mean that the poet's own 'voice' as such cannot be heard in the poems, but rather that it is *refracted* to varying degrees through the different languages the poems draw on; following Bakhtin, the word in *Crow*, 'breaking through to its own meaning and its own expression across an environment full of alien words and variously evaluating accents, harmonizing with some of the elements in this environment and striking a dissonance with others, is able, in this dialogized process, to shape its own stylistic profile and tone'[33]. That the 'stylistic profile' Hughes shapes for *Crow* is 'a super-simple and a super-ugly language' indicates that the book's key note is one of dissonance rather than of harmony: in an interview Hughes states: 'The first idea of *Crow* was really an idea of style. (. . .) The idea was originally just to write his songs, the songs that a Crow would sing. In other words, songs with no music whatsoever, in a super-simple and a super-ugly language which would in a way shed everything except just what he wanted to say without any other consideration and that's the basis of the style of the whole thing'[34]. The phrase 'shed everything' is telling: the impasse Crow must negotiate in these poems is (following Hughes's comments) essentially *discursive*, and would seem to stem from the inadequacy of cultural inscription (religious, mythical, scientific, popular) in the face of the 'living suffering spirit'[35] that Crow represents. In this respect, the formulaic patterns of many of the poems serve to foreground the *otherness* of the discursive materials (cartoons, the Bible) that are provided for Crow to represent himself, and it is significant that Crow inserts himself into a discursive frame only on condition of fiddling with its key elements (as in the biblical scenarios) and by bringing yet other discursive frames to bear (the 'low' language of cartoons). To read *Crow*'s words at face value is therefore to miss the point. Hughes's seemingly evasive comment that the poems 'wrote themselves'[36] is to be taken literally: the figure of Crow is as much as anything else a device for testing out cultural narratives and meanings that are already there, that have already been written; Crow does not so much produce meaning as re-accentuate it, blackly.

Crow's relationship to language is thematicized in a number of poems: 'Crow's First Lesson', 'A Disaster', 'The Battle of Osfrontalis', 'Crow Goes Hunting'. What these poems 'materialize' at the level of theme is the radical *otherness* of the word as experienced by Crow:

> Words came with Life Insurance policies —
> Crow feigned dead.
> Words came with warrants to conscript him —
> Crow feigned mad.
> Words came with blank cheques —
> He drew Minnie Mice on them.
>
> 'The Battle of Osfrontalis'

— etcetera. Figured as an agent of negativity with regard to the ideologically loaded word, Crow's only way forward in his quest for self-definition is through a kind of discursive loophole; this loophole is dialogical discourse as proposed by Bakhtin and elaborated by Kristeva: 'In its structures, writing reads another writing, reads itself and constructs itself through a process of destructive genesis'[37]. Neither cartoon nor bible story, neither poetry nor prose, *Crow* improvises its own dialogic space that is littered with the fragments of discursive collisions, collisions that concretize and relativize the 'mish-mash of scripture and physics' ('Crow's Account of the Battle') in and through which Crow is, in Hughes's words, 'intermittently conscious'[38].

On this reading — *Crow* as carnivalesque discourse — the book's violent and bizarre imagery involving bodily distortion and dismemberment is assimilable to Bakhtin's notion of the 'grotesque', defined by Bakhtin as 'The specific type of imagery inherent to the culture of folk humor in all its forms and manifestations'[39]. 'Material' processes of birth, death, copulation, growth, disintegration and dismemberment around which the grotesque bodily image gravitates are opposed by Bakhtin to 'the classic images of the finished, completed man, cleansed, as it were, of all the scoriae of birth and development'[40]. Seen in this light, the imagery of *Crow* seems to articulate a kind of grotesque ground swell (of bodily life), rupturing and denaturing the naturalized codes of Judaeo-Christian morality and Western scientific objectivism, codes that otherwise threaten to foreclose Crow's attempts to figure his own meaning.

Yet for all its indulgence in carnivalistic degradation, the language of *Crow* remains overtly devitalized, indifferent, expendable, void of affect. The book's formal reliance on the liturgical format seems only to reinforce the monotonous, arbitrary feel of it all. As Bedient notes, 'The attention [of the reader] soon stops dead like chalk hitting a wet spot on the board'[41]. Recourse to Bakhtin's ideas on 'carnivalesque' literature or 'dialogism', while being fully relevant to *Crow*, cannot finally account for this sort of language. It is enough to listen again to some of the more characteristic poem endings in order to hear how the carnival itself becomes reified, as if as the poems play themselves out they are simultaneously being distanced, devalued and discarded:

> But Crow only peered.
>   Then took a step or two forward,
> Grabbed this creature by the slackskin nape,
> Beat the hell out of it, and ate it.
>
>   'A Horrible Religious Error'

> And so the smile not even Leonardo
> Could have fathomed
> Flew off into the air, the rubbish heap of laughter
> Screams, discretions, indiscretions etcetera
>
>   'Crow Improvises'

> 'I give up,' he said. He gave up.
> Creation had failed again.
>
>   'A Bedtime Story'

> And everything goes to hell.
>
>   'Apple Tragedy'

> BANG!
> He was blasted to nothing.
>   'Truth Kills Everybody'

Hughes talks of the 'throwaway expressiveness'[42] of Shakespeare's language; on these terms, the language and tone here are simply 'throwaway'. Hughes's comment that in *Crow* he wanted to find 'a super-simple and a super-ugly language which would (. . .) shed everything', while pointing up the disenchanted, deadpan feel of the book's language, suggests also a kind of regression. Discussing what he refers to as the 'profound alienation of the subject in our scientific civilization', Lacan writes: 'If the subject did not rediscover in a regression — often pushed right back to the "mirror stage" — the enclosure of a stage in which his ego contains its imaginary exploits, there would hardly be any assignable limits to the credulity to which he must succumb (. . .)'[43]. It is a regression of this order that is suggested by the language and imagery of *Crow*, and which can be mapped theoretically with reference to Lacan's conception of the 'mirror stage' in child development.

THROUGH THE LOOKING GLASS

Bakhtin's idea of the 'typical "carnival anatomy" — an enumeration of the parts of the dismembered body'[44] finds a significant parallel in Lacan's identification of anxieties about bodily fragmentation present in the formation of the ego, anxieties revealed in dreams by certain psychically charged images Lacan terms '*imagos of the fragmented body*': 'images of castration, mutilation, dismemberment, dislocation, evisceration, devouring, bursting open of the body'[45]. These images, which both Lacan and Bakhtin find realized in the paintings of Hieronymus Bosch[46], pervade *Crow*:

> With here, brains in hands, for example,
> And there, legs in a treetop.
>   'Crow's Account of the Battle'

Lacan locates the genesis of these 'phantasmagorias'[47] at the mirror stage, a pivotal time in childhood between the ages of six and eighteen months when the child, 'still sunk in his motor incapacity and nursling dependence'[48], first comes to recognise his own image in a mirror. What is significant for Lacan is that this specular image, 'jubilantly' assumed by the child, 'situates the agency of the ego, before its social determination, in a fictional direction'[49]; in other words, the promise of bodily unity and coherence given in the virtual space of the mirror captivates the child and sets it in 'discordance with his own reality'[50], that is, the reality of the child's bodily uncoordination and helplessness at this time. This primary identification with an alienating mirage lays the ground for all secondary, what Lacan terms 'Imaginary' identifications through which the ego will determine itself: 'It is in this erotic relation, in which the human individual fixes upon himself an image that alienates him from himself, that are to be found the energy and the form on which this organization of the passions that he will call his ego is based'[51]. It is henceforth in the maintenance of what Lacan refers to as 'the armour of an alienating identity'[52], through the mechanics of identification, that Imaginary effects are manifested in the subject. The fantasy of the body 'in bits and pieces' is a kind of side-effect of the assumption of this 'armour', and is prone to erupt at moments of 'aggressive disintegration in the individual'[53].

Shamanic fantasies of death and dismemberment, in which Hughes interests himself and whose motifs can be found in all his major work, seem to belong to the same psychic terrain Lacan delineates here. It is in *Crow*, however, that this regression or disintegration is pushed back the farthest, to a stage where all attempted identifications fail and where language itself becomes reified to the point of apathy as Crow remains unable to solidify himself into any signifier or field of signifiers.

This regression as such would also help account for the enigmatic and at times grotesque images of laughter, smiling and grinning that occur throughout *Crow* ('I'm not quite sure what they signify' — Hughes). Kristeva locates the origin of laughter 'Chronologically and logically long before the mirror stage'[54]; Kelly Oliver sums up Kristeva's position: 'Prior to its constitution as a subject, let alone a speaking subject, the infant makes "music" as a direct release of drive. It expels sounds in order to release tension, either pain or pleasure, in order to survive. One such sound is laughter'[55]. As the infant begins to develop a sense of its own bodily coherence (the mirror stage), laughter becomes bound up with the confounding of this ideal: 'As we know, children lack a sense of humor (humor presupposes the superego and its bewildering). But they laugh easily when motor tension is linked to vision (a caricature is a visualiza- tion of bodily distortion, of an extreme, exaggerated movement, or of an unmastered movement); when a child's body is too rapidly set in motion by the adult (return to a motility defying its fixation, space, and place); when a sudden stop follows a movement (someone stumbles and falls)'[56]. When in *Crow* 'People's arms and legs fly off and fly on again/ In laughter' ('In Laughter'), the implication seems to be that an experiential space has been rediscovered — what Kristeva calls 'this archaic laughter-space'[57] — that defies the laws and logic of the known and constituted (a space reproduced in the cartoons *Crow* draws on).

While a poem like 'In Laughter' seems merely intent on celebrating this rediscovery, other instances of laughter in *Crow* generate more problematic implications:

His hands covered with blood suddenly
And now he ran from the children and ran through the house
Holding his bloody hands clear of everything
And ran along the road and into the wood
And under the leaves he sat weeping

And under the leaves he sat weeping

Till he began to laugh

'Criminal Ballad'

The enigmatic switch from weeping to laughing points to a 'bewildered' superego: a release of affective tension comes across that cannot find any social, religious or ethical code to legitimate itself; hence the poem's title. In its oblique way the poem registers a dissociation between affective life and the Western social contract, suggesting the bankruptcy of our religious and ethical systems.

Although the poems draw freely on the terms and concepts of psychoanalysis, these terms and concepts have no privileged hold on meaning here, as the savage parody of the Oedipus complex in 'Song for a Phallus' indicates. Equally, Hughes's own earlier poetry does not escape the rout:

Drinking Beowulf's blood, and wrapped in his hide,
Crow communes with poltergeists out of old ponds.

'Crowego'

Echoes of the Anglo–Saxon alliterative tradition in Hughes's first book *The Hawk in the Rain* (1957), the poet's interest in shamanism, the poetry as fishing metaphor in the early poem 'Pike' — all here seem absurd, no longer adequate to Hughes's meaning, which has now effectively overshot the limits of language.

Hughes describes Crow's adventures thus: 'Having been created, he's put through various adventures and disasters and trials and ordeals, and the effect of these is to alter him not at all, then alter him a great deal, completely transform him, tear him to bits, put him together again, and produce him a little bit changed. And maybe his ambition is to become a man, which he never quite manages'[58]. God's attempt to teach Crow how to talk in 'Crow's First Lesson' sets the pattern for the book: Crow's difficulty is that he cannot adapt to the alien discourses in which he finds himself placed, he cannot normalize himself within any single cultural code (in this case the Christian idea of God as Love) — hence his trials and ordeals. Some of the titles of the poems draw attention to the dilemma: 'Crow Tries the Media', 'Crow Paints Himself into a Chinese Mural'. In other words, Crow cannot become a man because he cannot identify with men, with what it means to be a man in Western society. Looking in the mirror 'For a glimpse of the usual grinning face' ('Crow's Vanity'), Crow is faced instead with fleeting, enigmatic images of burning gulfs and hanging gardens, as though the primary narcissistic identification, springboard for all secondary, social identifications, here found itself displaced by a fantasy of organic disarray. In short, the possibility of identification itself is suspended in *Crow*. Unable to settle within any language or idea, to fix the drives he embodies to available models of meaning, Crow can only utter an alien and empty language, a language that is felt to be meaningless. In so far as it can be read as an address to a Muse, the poem 'Littleblood', coming as it does at the end of the book, suggests that nothing with any truth value has as yet been said: 'Sit on my finger, sing in my ear, O littleblood.'

The problem with all this is that it sounds to an ear not similarly attuned like bad writing — Hughes ends up coming across as a total nihilist. Yet the advantage for the writer lies in the way the social contract — what Hughes refers to as 'the clutter of our civilized liberal confusion'[59] — is left unoccupied by any affect, suspended in mid-air, so to speak, its 'defiles' (Lacan's word[60]) realized as so many alienating detours from an ineffable primal truth, as so many displacements and deferments of what is at stake at the heart of the *I*. Crow's ransacking of history and culture attests to a quest for meaning other than the alienating meanings supported by a social and linguistic order that cannot hold him, an impossible conundrum — as paradoxical as Lacan's parodic reformulation of Descartes's 'I think, therefore I am': 'I think where I am not, therefore I am where I do not think'[61]. It is Crow's 'intermittent' subjection to language and culture — the Lacanian Symbolic order — that allows him to 'think' (to be 'intermittently conscious') along the lines that language and culture lay down; yet Crow also represents what is residual to and irreducible to language and culture: in so far as Crow embodies that which in the self eludes social and cultural inscription, he can thus only 'think' where he is not (i.e. in language). A kind of spanner in the Symbolic works, what Crow finally articulates, as his name connotes, is the primacy of what Freud designates as the most instinctual drive, the death drive[62], a drive which in Kristeva's words 'no signifier, no mirror, no other and no mother could ever contain'[63].

DEPRESSION: A STYLE

At least theoretically, regression to the mirror stage entails the risk of a collapse into cognitive chaos, even psychosis. Kristeva writes: 'Dreams of borderline patients, schizoid personalities, or those undergoing psychedelic experiments are often "abstract paintings" or cascades of sounds, intricacies of lines and fabrics, in which the analyst deciphers the dissociation — or a nonintegration — of psychic and somatic unity. Such indices could be interpreted as the ultimate imprint of the death drive. (. . .) the work of death as such, at the zero degree of psychicism, can be spotted precisely in the *dissociation of form* itself, when form is distorted, abstracted, disfig-ured, hollowed out: ultimate thresholds of inscribable dislocation and jouissance . . .'[64]. The disfigured and abstracted language of *Crow* clearly bears some relation to what Kristeva describes here; on the other hand, *Crow*'s 'hollowed out' language is not unreadable. It still signifies, even if what is signified is felt in the end to be neither here nor there. In this respect, what supports the subject of *Crow* when all identificatory support is lost is the wave of affect that constitutes *depression* (Freud incidentally designates the melancholy person's superego as a 'cultivation of death drive'[65]). According to Kristeva: 'Unlike what happens with psychotics, (. . .) depressed persons do not forget how to use signs. They keep them, but the signs seem absurd, delayed, ready to be extinguished, (. . .) As for the discourse of the depressed, it is the "normal" surface of a psychotic risk: the sadness that overwhelms us, the retardation that paralyzes us are also a shield — sometimes the last one — against madness'[66]. Withdrawing from its desiring bonds to the other and to language, it is as if the depressed subject takes refuge in a cushion of mood that breaks a potentially devas-tating fall through the mirror: alluding to Lacan's concept of the mirror stage (the child's 'jubilatory assumption' of its reflected image), Kristeva writes of how 'Depressive denial (. . .) affects even the possibilities of a *representation of narcissistic coherence*, hence depriving the subject of its auto-erotic exultation, of its "jubilatory assumption" '[67]. Following this fall: '(. . .) sadness reconstitutes an affective cohesion of the self, which restores its unity within the framework of the affect. The depressive mood constitutes itself as a narcissistic support, negative to be sure, but nevertheless present-ing the self with an integrity, nonverbal though it might be. Because of that, the depressive affect makes up for symbolic invalidation and inter-ruption (the depressive's "that's meaningless") and at the same time protects it against proceeding to the suicidal act'[68]. A. Alvarez's comment, chosen for the blurb on the book's cover, is in an inadvertent way close to the bone of *Crow*: 'Each fresh encounter with despair becomes the occasion for a separate, almost funny, story in which natural forces and creatures, mythic figures, even parts of the body, act out their special roles (. . .)'[69]. That is, the poems function as so many attempts to get a potentially debilitating 'encounter with despair' back on the Symbolic move, to fix it in a rep-resentation, a move that none the less repeatedly falls through itself as the chosen signifier or field of signifiers proves to be too flimsy for the task. However, this is not the same as saying that the poems fail as poems. Almost despite himself, Calvin Bedient notices how a kind of affective meaning is conveyed in the poems through the very *insignificance* of their language: 'At this stage of case-hardened disillusion, so Hughes seems to say, words will all taste the same anyhow. The very indifference of the language is thus expressive'[70].

What linguistics and literary theory teach us about the arbitrary nature of language is in a sense glaringly obvious to the depressed subject, a subject who is positioned through what Kristeva terms 'the denial of negation':

> Listen again for a few moments to depressive speech, repetitive, monotonous, or empty of meaning, inaudible even for the speaker before he or she sinks into mutism. You will note that, with melancholy persons, meaning appears to be arbitrary, or else it is elaborated with the help of much knowledge and will to mastery, but seems secondary, frozen, somewhat removed from the head and body of the person who is speaking. Or else it is from the very beginning evasive, uncertain, deficient, quasi mutistic: 'one' speaks to you already convinced that the words are wrong and therefore 'one' speaks carelessly, 'one' speaks without believing in it.
>
> Meaning, however, is arbitrary; linguistics asserts it for all verbal signs and for all discourse. Is not the signifier LAF completely unmotivated with respect to the meaning of 'laugh,' and also, and above all, with respect to the act of laughing, its physical production, its intrapsychic and interreactional value? (. . .) Now every 'normal' speaker learns to take that artifice seriously, to cathex it or forget it.
>
> Signs are arbitrary because language starts with a *negation* of loss, along with the depression occasioned by mourning. 'I have lost an essential object that happens to be, in the final analysis, my mother,' is what the speaking being seems to be saying. 'But no, I have found her again in signs, or rather since I consent to lose her I have not lost her (that is the negation), I can recover her in language.'
>
> Depressed persons, on the contrary, *disavow the negation:* they cancel it out, suspend it, and nostalgically fall back on the real object (the Thing) of their loss, which is just what they do not manage to lose, to which they remain painfully riveted. The *denial of negation* would thus be the exercise of an impossible mourning, the setting up of a fundamental sadness and an artificial, unbelievable language, cut out of the painful background that is not accessible to any signifier and that intonation alone, intermittently, succeeds in inflecting.[71]

What Hughes refers to in a typically esoteric manner as Crow's bride — 'What Crow is grappling with is (. . .) what becomes — at the end of his mistakes and errantry — his bride and his almost-humanity'[72] — is less an object of desire than the depressive's unsignifiable 'Thing', the very 'seat of the sexuality from which the object of desire will become separated'[73]. It is this Thing that Crow tries to recover in signs. It is the 'soul' of 'Two Legends', 'the huge stammer/ Of the cry that, swelling, could not/ Pronounce its sun'. It is the 'egg of blackness' of the same poem from which Crow is hatched into 'emptiness' — the lack-ridden language of the poems — much as the object of desire separates itself from the seat of the Thing. Yet Crow is no object of desire, only a provisional device for trying to establish such an object, a quest in which, shackled as he is to his Thing, Crow stumbles, fails, falls to pieces. The poems in this sense are no more than varyingly 'unsuccessful' attempts to translate this unnameable affect which Crow represents.

However, to simply point out that *Crow* is about depression would be as banal as pronouncing Hughes a nihilist, and the point would not be worth mentioning were it not for the light that a psychoanalytic understanding of depression is able to throw on to the problematic question of the book's style and technique. In short, to comprehend the de-alienating mechanics of depressive withdrawal is to grasp the meaning of *Crow*. Kristeva writes of how 'The surge of affect and primary semiotic processes comes into conflict, in depressive persons, with the linguistic armor (. . .) as well as with symbolic constructs (apprenticeships, ideologies, beliefs)'[74]. When words come with Life Insurance policies for Crow, he feigns dead, and so on. What Lacan calls 'the armour of an alienating identity' here has no hold, it is 'shed'. In Kristeva's words, 'translation — our fate as speaking beings' has here stopped 'its vertiginous course toward metalanguages or foreign languages, which are like many sign systems distant from the site of pain'[75] (although the poem 'The Black Beast' does see Crow sitting in the Black Beast's chair, 'telling loud lies against the Black Beast' — Crow is of course a black beast — in this case ironically signalling the alienating destination of Crow as rational inquirer). This is the same point that Lacan makes when he warns of the 'credulity' to which the subject who does not regress is prone. It is this regressive stage where Crow walks and muses in the poem 'A Disaster', where earth's people are 'All digested inside the word'. Similarly, in 'The Battle of Osfrontalis', words have taken 'the whole world with them — / But the world did not notice'. Cipher of an 'inalienable, inseparable, and for that very reason, unnameable' affect[76], Crow remains (to some extent) word-resistant, although he *does* notice what words can do; it is thus to his Thing that Crow owes his metaphysical lucidity. Kristeva writes:

> (. . .) the sequence of linguistic representations, dissociated as it might be from drive-related and affective representatives, can assume with depressed persons considerable associative originality, (. . .) The psychomotor

retardation of depressive persons may be accompanied, contrary to
appearances of passivity, by an accelerated, creative cognitive process —
witness the studies bearing on the very singular and inventive associations
made by depressed persons starting from word lists submitted to them.
Such hyperactivity with signifiers reveals itself particularly by connecting
distant semantic fields and recalls the puns of hypomaniacs. It is
coextensive with the cognitive hyperlucidity of depressed persons,
but also with the manic-depressive's inability to decide or choose.

(. . .) certain forms of depression are bouts of associative accelerations
that destabilize the subject and afford it an escape route away from
confrontation with a stable signification or a steady object.[77]

The flat, carnivalistic jumble of incongruous discourses in *Crow* constitutes
just such an escape route from a social and cultural system that is felt to
be unable to do justice to the self.

Still, it does not follow that the poems in *Crow* are meaningless: only
that the language of the poems, its referential function displaced, must be
taken as an object of representation in itself before its meaning as such can
be heard. 'Crow's Account of the Battle' refers the reader less to any battle
than to the available means of representing and responding to the event.
The cascade of phrases and clichés that have here become dislocated from
their semantic fields — science, children's fiction, the cartoon-strip, and
in particular the television or newspaper report — registers the traumatic
(in the sense of *intractable*) nature of the site of pain. Referring to the
emergence of 'the gas chambers, the atomic bomb, [and] the gulag' in the
Second World War, Kristeva writes: 'What those monstrous and painful
sights do damage to are our systems of perception and representation. As
if overtaxed or destroyed by too powerful a breaker, our symbolic means
find themselves hollowed out, nearly wiped out, paralyzed'[78]. Similarly,
Hughes writes of the 'plunge into the new dimension' that was the First
World War, 'where suddenly and for the first time Adam's descendants
found themselves meaningless'[79]. If a poem like 'Crow's Account of the
Battle' can be said to bear meaning, it is a meaning that opens not onto
the possibility of signification but is instead generated by a signifying
crisis. The arbitrary concatenations here register a traumatized inability to
concatenate meaningfully. Kristeva writes: 'The affected rhetoric of litera-
ture and even the common rhetoric of everyday speech always seem some-
what festive. How can one speak the truth of pain, if not by holding in
check the rhetorical celebration, warping it, making it grate, strain, and
limp?'[80]. The type of awkward, mangled language to be found in *Crow*
might be the only authentic way of articulating this pain, a pain which
releases the subject into a 'deep narcissism, the archaic autosensuality of
wounded affects'[81].

NOTES

1. Roy Fuller, 'Views', *The Listener* vol. 85, 11 March 1971, p. 297.
2. Geoffrey Thurley, *The Ironic Harvest: English Poetry in the Twentieth Century* (London: Arnold, 1974), p. 189.
3. Calvin Bedient, *Eight Contemporary Poets* (London: Oxford University Press, 1974), pp. 101, 114.
4. *Ibid.*, p. 114.
5. Mikhail Bakhtin, *Problems of Dostoevsky's Poetics* ed. and trans. Caryl Emerson (Manchester: Manchester University Press, 1984), p. 123.
6. Ted Hughes, 'A Reply to Critics', in A. E. Dyson (ed.), *Three Contemporary Poets: Thom Gunn, Ted Hughes and R. S. Thomas: A Casebook* (Basingstoke: Macmillan, 1990), p. 112.
7. Paul Radin, *The Trickster: A Study in American Indian Mythology* (New York: Schocken, 1972), p. xxiv.
8. 'Ted Hughes's *Crow*', *The Listener* 30th July 1970, p. 149.
9. Radin, p. xxiv.
10. Bakhtin, *Problems of Dostoevsky's Poetics*, p. 107.
11. Hughes, 'A Reply to Critics', p. 110.
12. Mikhail Bakhtin, *Rabelais and his World* trans. Hélène Iswolsky (Cambridge, Mass.: MIT Press, 1968), p. 11.
13. *Ibid.*, p. 6.
14. Hughes, 'A Reply to Critics', p. 110.
15. Bakhtin, *Rabelais and his World*, p. 19.
16. Mikhail Bakhtin, *The Dialogic Imagination: Four Essays by M. M. Bakhtin* ed. Michael Holquist, trans. Caryl Emerson and Michael Holquist (Austin: U of Texas P, 1981), p. 21.
17. Ekbert Faas, 'Ted Hughes and *Crow*', Interview with Ted Hughes, *London Magazine* vol. 10 no. 10, January 1971, p. 18.
18. Bakhtin, *Rabelais and his World*, p. 20.
19. Bakhtin, *The Dialogic Imagination*, p. 23.
20. Faas, p. 18.
21. Jonathan Raban, *The Society of the Poem* (London: Harrap, 1971), p. 166.
22. Radin, p. 168.
23. Ted Hughes, *Winter Pollen: Occasional Prose* ed. William Scammell (London: Faber, 1994), p. 129.
24. David Lodge, *Working with Structuralism: Essays and Reviews on Nineteenth- and Twentieth-Century Literature* (London: Routledge, 1981), pp. 171–172.
25. *Ibid.*, p. 173.
26. C. G. Jung, 'On the Psychology of the Trickster Figure', in Radin, p. 205.
27. Ted Hughes, 'Myth and Education', in *Children's Literature in Education* 1, 1970, p. 58.
28. *Ibid.*, p. 68.
29. Hughes, *Winter Pollen*, p. 226.
30. Bakhtin, *The Dialogic Imagination*, p. 301.
31. *Ibid.*, p. 299.
32. *Ibid.*, p. 76.

33. *Ibid.*, p. 277.
34. Faas, p. 20.
35. Hughes uses the phrase in connection with Popa's poetry, in *Winter Pollen*, p. 221.
36. Faas, p. 18.
37. Julia Kristeva, *Desire in Language: A Semiotic Approach to Literature and Art* ed. Leon S. Roudiez, trans. Thomas Gora, Alice Jardine and Leon S. Roudiez (Oxford: Blackwell, 1981), p. 77.
38. Hughes, 'A Reply to Critics', p. 111.
39. Bakhtin, *Rabelais and his World*, p. 30.
40. *Ibid.*, p. 25.
41. Bedient, p. 116.
42. Faas, p. 13.
43. Jacques Lacan, *Écrits: A Selection* trans. Alan Sheridan (London: Tavistock/Routledge, 1977), p. 70.
44. Bakhtin, *Problems of Dostoevsky's Poetics*, p. 102.
45. Lacan, *Écrits*, p. 11.
46. See *ibid.*, pp. 4–5 and Bakhtin, *Rabelais and his World*, p. 27.
47. Lacan, *Écrits*, p. 12.
48. *Ibid.*, p. 2.
49. *Ibid.*, p. 2.
50. *Ibid.*, p. 2.
51. *Ibid.*, p. 19.
52. *Ibid.*, p. 4.
53. *Ibid.*, p. 4.
54. Kristeva, *Desire in Language*, p. 283.
55. Kelly Oliver, *Reading Kristeva: Unraveling the Double-bind* (Bloomington: Indiana University Press, 1993), p. 35.
56. Kristeva, *Desire in Language*, p. 284.
57. *Ibid.*, p. 285.
58. 'Ted Hughes's Crow', p. 149.
59. Hughes, *Winter Pollen*, p. 221.
60. Lacan writes of human needs and desires having to 'pass through the defiles of the signifier'; *Écrits*, p. 264.
61. *Ibid.*, p. 166.
62. J. Laplanche and J.-B. Pontalis write: 'This instinct is held to represent the fundamental tendency of every living being to return to the inorganic state (. . .) Freud looks upon these (. . .) instincts as the instincts *par excellence*, in that they typify the repetitive nature of instinct in general'; *The Language of Psycho-Analysis* trans. Donald Nicholson-Smith (London: Karnac, 1988), pp. 97, 98.
63. Julia Kristeva, *The Kristeva Reader* ed. Toril Moi (Oxford: Blackwell, 1986), p. 103.
64. Julia Kristeva, *Black Sun: Depression and Melancholia* trans. Leon S. Roudiez (New York: Columbia University Press, 1989), p. 27.
65. *Ibid.*, p. 17.
66. *Ibid.*, pp. 47, 42.
67. *Ibid.*, p. 49.
68. *Ibid.*, p. 19.
69. Blurb on back cover to Ted Hughes, *Crow: From the Life and Songs of the Crow* (London: Faber, 1970, 1972).

70. Bedient, p. 114.
71. Kristeva, *Black Sun*, pp. 43–44.
72. Ted Hughes, 'On Images in *Crow*', in Dyson, p. 114.
73. Kristeva, *Black Sun*, p. 13.
74. *Ibid.*, pp. 64–65.
75. *Ibid.*, p. 42.
76. *Ibid.*, p. 240.
77. *Ibid.*, p. 59.
78. *Ibid.*, p. 223.
79. Hughes, *Winter Pollen*, p. 72.
80. Kristeva, *Black Sun*, p. 225.
81. *Ibid.*, p. 240.

CHAPTER THREE

Gaudete

'SOME KIND OF TUNNEL'

Referring to the narrative of *Gaudete* (1977), Hughes remarks how 'at every point the intonation of the language becomes infected by the tempo and style of whatever character it's dealing with at the time'[1]. Intrusive narrative commentary is absent from the text: 'Various people in the book give their opinions, in various tones of voice, which I indicate. My own opinion I withhold. It's like a play — it contains no author's comments. As far as interpretation goes — I leave all options open'[2]. The narrative's shifting viewpoint, devoid of authorial commentary, in a sense engages the reader in events; as Bakhtin writes of Dostoevsky's 'polyphonic novel': 'It is constructed not as the whole of a single consciousness, absorbing other consciousnesses as objects into itself, but as a whole formed by the interaction of several consciousnesses, none of which entirely becomes an object for the other; this interaction provides no support for the viewer who would objectify an entire event according to some ordinary mono-logic category (thematically, lyrically or cognitively) — and this conse-quently makes the viewer also a participant. (. . .) Not a single element of the work is structured from the point of view of a non–participating "third person" '[3]. In the narrative of *Gaudete*, the 'non–participating third person' is constituted only fleetingly: we are told, for instance, that Hagen, watching Lumb and his wife through binoculars, 'does not detect/ Lumb's absence' (p. 25); again, at the orgy at the women's institute we are told of Felicity that 'In the lottery of the mushroom sandwich/ Everything was arranged for her' (p. 140). In both cases the reader is given information that appears not to be refracted through one or another of the characters' eyes[4]. However, in both cases the omniscient position is no sooner established than it dissolves: the narrator's comment on Hagen leads into the 'darkness' into which Hagen's wife 'has squeezed her eyes' (p. 25), while the information about Felicity is followed by Felicity's own experience of her mushroom trip: 'What she has eaten and drunk/ Is flying her through great lights and dropping her from gulf to gulf' (p. 140). The omniscient 'third person', where present, seems only to constitute an *edge* over which a dissolve may occur; far from enabling a stable, 'nonparticipating' view of events, it is as if the authoritative position (where this position is to be found in the first place) were set up only to be overturned among a shifting succession of viewpoints (it does not *frame* or *bind* the narrative).

This is no doubt part of what Hughes means when he describes his intention in *Gaudete*:

> (. . .) I became (. . .) interested in doing a headlong narrative. Something like a Kleist story that would go from beginning to end in some forceful way pushing the reader through some kind of tunnel while being written in the kind of verse that would stop you dead at every moment. A great driving force meeting solid resistance. And in order to manage that I had to enclose myself within a very narrow tone, almost a monotone, so that the actual narrative trimmed itself down more and more.[5]

The narrative 'tunnel' of *Gaudete* — the absence of an authoritative overview of events — is reflected at the level of theme: the ubiquity of the lens in the main narrative — perspectives are presented through binoculars, telescopes, gunsights and the 'objective' evidence of a photograph — suggests not only the experiential detachment of the village men, but also their desire to attain a distanced, objective perspective on events: the narrative implicates the one in the other. The reader is alerted to the importance of the lens in the main narrative by the opening word: 'Binoculars'. The primarily visual nature of the narrative (originally intended as a film script) and its complete absence of dialogue lends it something of the quality of a silent movie. When Hagen shoots his dog in a rage at his wife's infidelity with Lumb's double, his wife looks on 'As if it were all something behind the nearly unbreakable screen glass of a television/ With the sound turned off' (p. 35). Similarly, through his telescope Estridge watches his daughter 'screaming something at him/ As if in perfect silence' (p. 48). In 'trimming' the narrative of intrusive commentary Hughes in effect turns the sound down, so that the reader, like the characters themselves, cannot be sure what to make of events.

LENS AND LANDSCAPE

The clipped brevity of the noun-phrases through which Hagen is introduced emphasizes his detached inertia: 'Major Hagen, motionless at a window, / As in a machan,/ Shoulders hunched, at a still focus' (p. 23). In contrast to the 'still focus' of Hagen (we find out he is watching his wife with Lumb's double), the landscape of the scene is ebulliently and unmanageably active, a site of verbal fluidity and collision rather than of orderly noun-phrases:

> The parkland unrolls, lush with the full ripeness of the last week in May, under the wet midmorning light. The newly plumped grass shivers and flees. Giant wheels of light ride into the chestnuts, and the poplars lift and pour like the tails of horses. Distance blues beyond distance.
>
> (p. 23)

The interplay between such metaphorically energetic and fluid evocations of the May landscape and the 'still focus' of the lenses through which the men (and by extension the reader) orient themselves in relation to it is one of the ways in which the narrative thematicizes the 'great driving force meeting solid resistance' Hughes is aiming for (the other is the effect the duplicate vicar has on his parishioners).

In effect, the focalizing lenses of the main narrative are constantly displaced by a pull towards disorientation and fragmentation represented by the landscape. The lens metonymically suggests the centripetal force of consciousness itself, attempting to focus itself in relation to a centrifugal flux of experiential data. When Hagen shoots the dove after observing his wife and Lumb's double together, Garten overhears the shot: 'He pinpoints it. He identifies it. He judges Hagen has shot a woodpigeon on his morning walk' (p. 29). The drama of the scene lies in the dialectic it sets in motion between Garten's predilection for pinpointing/identifying/judging and the way the landscape seems to 'start up' again after the act of focalization: 'The wood creeps rustling back. The million whispering busyness of the fronds, which seem to have hesitated, start up their stitchwork, with clicking of stems and all the tiny excitements of their materials' (p. 29). The reader is channelled along Garten's objective, categorizing, interpretative viewpoint only to encounter dissolution and entropy at the far end. The narrative is in this sense open at the seams: the reader, in conjunction with the men, is both detached voyeur of the silent events sealed off on the far side of the various lenses (and lens-like consciousnesses) through which they are viewed (the pervasive silence suggesting the experiential dislocation of the characters), while at the same time undergoing the fragmentation and disorientation of the lens's focus (the absence of an authoritative, controlling overview through which the 'meaning' of events can be made clear).

Hughes's 'prose-readiness' with the long line in the narrative constitutes a means of tugging against the 'leash' of the voyeuristic, controlling gaze of the men:

> The vista quivers.
> Decorative and ordered, it tugs at a leash.
> A purplish turbulence
> Boils from the stirred chestnuts, and the spasms of the new grass, and the dark
> nodes of bulls.
>
> (p. 26)

Gaudete stages this dialectic between centripetal focus and centrifugal 'turbulence' on all levels. At the beginning of the book, a number of intertextual frames are pointed up as potential interpretative guidelines — in particular folklore ('Just as in the Folktale', Argument [p. 9]) and myth (the quotes from Heraclitus and *Parzival* that face the Argument) — none of which seem adequately to bind the narrative on their own terms; the narrative overspills its own frames, as it were, shifting and mixing codes in a way that shoulders off the reader's desire for narrative and thematic coherence: self-consciously placing itself within the tradition of popular/pulp 'realist' fiction (from which the book's blatant character stereotypes are drawn: 'A lecherous priest and a gaggle of spoofed women. Hysterical bored country wives. Credulous unfortunate females' [p. 128]), the narrative nevertheless never hesitates to borrow from other genres and codes, be it the crude imagery and diction of contemporary horror films/fiction — 'The jaws loll, as he lifts strengthless heads, which drop back slack-necked' (p. 11) — or the hyperbolic excesses of Gothic — 'And thunder trundles continually around the perimeter of the deeply padded heaven/ And through the cellars of the lake/ With splittings of giant trees and echoing of bronze flues and mazy corridors' (p. 81). Towards the close of the main narrative, the touch of melodrama in the description of 'The hunchbacked bullet' escaping 'among lily-roots' (p. 168) hints at the poet's own semantic getaway behind the intertextual thicket of his language, leaving the reader with an unresolved tangle of textual threads yet without the necessary authorial support to tie them up, much as the 'sodden paper' Lumb's double is handed at one point 'as if it were some explanation' (p. 100) disintegrates in the elemental onslaught.

THE USE OF STEREOTYPES

As a fable of the incompletion and fluidity of bodily and unconscious life (as pitted against the repressive, normalizing agency of cultural codes and taboos), the narrative remains irreconcilable to the tradition of popular realist fiction within which it is nevertheless situated by its conspicuous use of character stereotypes. Gifford and Roberts find this use damaging: the narrative for them is 'grossly reliant on caricature and the stereotypes of an outdated popular fiction'[6]. However, this reliance is if anything foregrounded, making little pretence to transparency (realism): as if it were a toby jug, Hagen's face wears 'A perfunctory campaign leatheriness. / A frontal Viking weatherproof/ Drained of the vanities, pickled in mess-alcohol and smoked dark' (p. 24). The description emboldens the contours of the character to the point at which any potential character development is foreclosed: the character is fixed within his own characterological code.

As Gifford and Roberts note, in *Gaudete* Hughes does not seem to be concerned with the 'continuity and extension' of his characters' lives[7]. It is as if the characters here were being set up merely for a fall: the primary focus in the narrative seems to be on what might be designated as characterological *rupture*; that is, on experiences disruptive of and unassimilable to character type (i.e. unassimilable to consciousness: Lacan designates the trauma as an experience which is fundamentally 'unassimilable'; in Lacanian terms, the trauma — around which *Gaudete* is at times explicitly focused — thus comes at the subject from the Real[8]). Neil Roberts makes the point that as the men in the narrative 'are very clearly constructed out of a limited number of key motifs, and these motifs are repeated in different characters', the things that happen to them happen 'as if to a single person, and at the end they react as a single person'[9]. This reading is supported by Hughes's own comment that he initially planned to make the narrative Hagen's story — 'A story of what's going on in his head'[10]. On this reading — the male characters as aspects of a single male consciousness — what remains central to Hughes's concern is the effect on this consciousness of the traumatic happenings it is confronted with: 'what's going on in his head'.

Craig Robinson writes of the stereotype in *Gaudete*: 'It is part of Hughes' point that the men of the village are most of the time empty, flat stereotypes, and only fill out in moments of crisis such as Lumb provides, and even then in a way unconnected with richness of character'[11]. *Fragment* would perhaps constitute a better description than 'fill out': at the traumatic moment of discovering Lumb's double with his wife, Dunworth is thrown into what is depicted as a kind of infantile confusion: unable to gather himself together (to act according to characterological dictates) — 'He gropes for his lost initiative, / But what he sees, like a surprising blow in a dark room, / Has scattered him' (p. 85) — he is released into 'his child's helplessness' (p. 87).

THE DOUBLE

The changeling himself is strikingly akin to the 'strange creature' Hughes finds at the heart of János Pilinszky's poetry: ' "a gasping, limbless trunk", savaged by primal hungers, among the odds and ends of a destroyed culture, waiting to be shot, or beaten to death, or just thrown on a refuse heap'[12]. In effect Lumb's double constitutes a grotesque materialization of the split in the self that is divined in Hughes's early poetry and that gave rise to the figure of Crow. As with Crow, the double's 'log-like' nature renders him unassimilable to the social order: as an 'emissary' of bodily life (Hughes refers to the characters' bodies in the story as 'emissaries'[13]), the double wreaks a kind of Dionysian havoc in the parish. His efficacy lies in the effect he has on other characters, the way his sexual antics puncture the network of norms and conventions and taboos that holds their world in place: Mrs. Westlake returns from a liaison with the duplicate Lumb to find her world has slipped its moorings: 'She finds herself now in one room, now in another, with a sensation of dropping through papery floors, falling from world to world' (p. 39). Lumb's actions tear through the fabric of the characters' habitual lives as though it were paper, exposing its fragility. As 'emissary' of a pressing bodily reality beyond the ken of consciousness, the double is an embodiment of the 'driving force meeting solid resistance' that Hughes locates at the heart of the text. Hughes writes:

> (. . .) what I held in focus as I wrote was a sense of the spirit energy staggering through the crassness of the living cells, in this group, and emerging in its way as stupefied and benighted, and going about its mission almost somnambulist, almost unconscious, tinkering with Heath-Robinson paper-back magical operations as an instinctive but muddled attempt to re-establish contact with the real origins and the real calling. The battery image of the poem was of transcendental energy jammed — unconscious and deformed in the collision — into dead-end objects, dead-end claustrophobic egos, dilettante museum egos, second-hand bailer-twine repaired mechanical egos, and galvanising them in perfunctory fashion blowing their inadequate circuits. (. . .) As if the brilliant real thing were happening to creatures of light in another

> world — but these are the shadows of it, confusedly glimpsing and
> remembering, translating it all into puppet and monkey and routine
> reflex, and helpless to manage even that, broken or demonised by
> the flashes of it, enmired in bodily thickness and ego inertia, and
> overwhelmed anyway by the vegetable weight and confusion and
> dumb beauty of late May.[14]

'Jammed' by the ego, 'enmired in bodily thickness', ineffably beyond com-
prehension: Hughes's use of the term 'real' here — 'the real origins and the
real calling . . . the brilliant real thing' — is directly analogous to the Lacanian
Real. Like Hughes, Lacan relates the human subject to the Real on the
level of psychosomatic: 'It's a relation to something which always lies on
the edge of our conceptual elaborations, which we are always thinking about,
which we sometimes speak of, and which, strictly speaking, we can't grasp,
and which is nonetheless there, don't forget it — I talk about the symbolic,
about the imaginary, but there is also the real. Psychosomatic relations are
at the level of the real'[15]. Like Crow — 'the hierophant, humped, impenet-
rable' ('Crow Communes') — Lumb's double is in a sense the body itself,
'a gasping, limbless trunk', as solidly insistent as it is ineffable.

LANGUAGE AND THE DOUBLE

One passage in particular enigmatically locates the dynamics of Lumb's split
with his double within the self's relation to 'other voices':

> Voices shut him in.
> He sees up through a spiralling stair of voices
> Into the sun's blaze cupola.
> He recognizes voices out of his past.
> Peremptory trivial phrases,
> Distinct and sudden, behind him and beside him.
> One voice is coming clearer, insistent.
> It calls his name repeatedly, searchingly.
> It is his own voice.
> As the other voices thicken over him
> He manages, as from his deep listening, to answer: 'I'm here.'
>
> (p. 77)

'I'm here' is conspicuous, constituting one of the only two instances of
directly reported speech in the narrative (the other instance is when Evans
shouts 'Bloody Hell!' during the final chase scene towards the close of the
narrative [p. 161]). Given 'the other voices' that seem to crowd out Lumb's

sense of self here, the words at first appear to tentatively signal Lumb's finding his 'own voice'. Yet it is significant that they are soon followed by the unexpected and jarring emergence of a double from the lake — unexpected because, chronologically at least, the Lumb whose thoughts are given here is already a double, the original Lumb having been abducted by elemental spirits in the Prologue. The double who appears at this point serves a kind of grotesque reminder of Lumb's inability to return himself to himself in language. Lumb's attempt to affirm his 'own voice' is in this light fraught with contradiction, seeming in retrospect like a flat capitulation to the otherness of 'Peremptory trivial phrases' — the phrase 'I'm here' sounds bathetically commonplace — a capitulation that precipitates the irreducible residuum of the double.

The double's defeat by the social order — his murder at the hands of the men of the village — is anticipated in the Argument, which locates the double's cancellation by the spirits at the point at which 'he begins to feel a nostalgia for independent, ordinary human life, free of his peculiar destiny' (p. 9). What is revealed as the double's 'favourite meditation' centres around this nostalgia at the same time as it suggests the double's irreducibility to any single life:

And tries to imagine simple freedom —
His possible freedoms, his other lives, hypothetical and foregone, his lost
        freedoms.
As each person carries the whole world, like a halo,
Albeit a dim and mostly provisional world, but with a brightly focused centre,
        under the sun,
Considering their millions
All mutually exclusive, all conjunct and co-extensive,
He sees in among them,
In among all the tiny millions of worlds of this world
Millions of yet other, alternative worlds, uninhabited, unnoticed, still empty,
Each open at every point to every other and yet distinct,
Each waiting for him to escape into it, to explore it and possess it,
Each with a bed at the centre. A name. A pair of shoes. And a door.
And surrounded by still-empty, never-used limitless freedom.
He yields to his favourite meditation.
Forlorn, desperate meditation.

                    (p. 50)

Gravitating towards the centripetal pull of the objects in which the ego sees its centrality mirrored — 'a bed at the centre. A name. A pair of shoes. And a door' (the list recalls the image in 'Stations': 'And his jacket, and his wife, and his last pillow/ Clung to each other') — the double's meditation (a kind of sublimation of his grotesquely overblown sexual appetite) at the same time outstrips by imaginatively multiplying his possible selves. The meditation is 'forlorn' in its circularity; wherever it rests the confines of the ego hover, ready to coagulate. The syntax of the passage enacts the 'desperate' ambivalence of the double's desire, the centrifugal proliferation of subordinate clauses, accentuated by the repetitive weave of diction ('freedom . . . freedoms . . . other . . . freedoms . . . world . . . world . . . millions . . . All . . . all . . . in among . . . In among . . . millions of worlds of this world/ Millions . . . other . . . worlds . . . Each . . . every . . . every other . . . Each . . . Each . . . freedom'), 'forlornly' pulling against the inevitable grammatical closure of the sentence. The overtly abstract and repetitive diction which buoys up the whole description has a curious effect: the word 'freedom' comes to feel semantically weightless, 'empty', an existential illusion that bars Lumb's double from awakening to the (unconscious) subjection of his desire to the 'otherness' of social constructions: 'A name. A pair of shoes. And a door.'

'ADVENTURE TIME' IN *GAUDETE*

In his role as harbinger of a bodily Real, Lumb's double, like the Dostoevskian hero as defined by Bakhtin, is in a sense placeless:

> The plot of the biographical novel is not adequate to Dostoevsky's hero, for such a plot relies wholly on the social and characterological definitiveness of the hero, on his full embodiment in life. Between the character of the hero and the plot of his life there must be a deep and organic unity. The biographical novel is built on it. The hero and the objective world surrounding him must be made of one piece. But Dostoevsky's hero in this sense is not embodied and cannot be embodied. He cannot have a normal biographical plot. The heroes themselves, it turns out, fervently dream of being embodied, they long to attach themselves to one of life's normal plots.[16]

Bakhtin here could equally be describing the basis of the double's 'favourite meditation' in *Gaudete*, his 'nostalgia for . . . ordinary human life'. Bakhtin links this distinguishing feature of the Dostoevskian hero — his *un*embodiment in any 'normal biographical plot' — to the 'plot-compositional base' of the European adventure tale:

> Between the adventure hero and the Dostoevskian hero there is one formal similarity, very fundamental to the structure of the novel. As regards the adventure hero also, it is impossible to say who he is. He has no firm socially typical or individually characterological qualities out of which a stable image of his character, type, or temperament might be

composed. Such a definitive image would weigh down the adventure plot, limit the adventure possibilities. To the adventure hero anything can happen, he can become anything. He too is not a substance, but a pure function of adventures and escapades. The adventure hero is, to the same degree as Dostoevsky's hero, not finalized and not predetermined by his image.[17]

Like the European adventure hero, Lumb's double operates more as grotesque 'function' rather than characterological 'substance' — a function comically pointed up by the farcically unrealistic succession of sexual liaisons he manages to improvise within a single day (the rapid chain of events in the narrative takes place in a kind of dream-time, not the everyday time of realism[18]).

'Adventure-time' is defined by Bakhtin in the following way: 'In this kind of time, nothing changes: the world remains as it was, the biographical life of the heroes does not change, their feelings do not change, people do not even age. This empty time leaves no traces anywhere, no indications of its passing. This (. . .) is an extratemporal hiatus that appears between two moments of a real time sequence (. . .)'[19]. Just as 'Moments of adventuristic time occur at those points when the normal course of events, the normal, intended or purposeful sequence of life's events is interrupted'[20], so the main narrative of Gaudete takes place between the abduction and re-appearance of Lumb. Bakhtin notes how 'These points provide an opening for the intrusion of nonhuman forces — fate, gods, villains — and it is precisely these forces, and not the heroes, who in adventure-time take all the initiative'[21]. In having Lumb 'carried away' by elemental spirits, Hughes seems overtly to draw on the tradition outlined by Bakhtin (one of the two quotations that frame the narrative is from Parzival, which Bakhtin refers to as an example of the kind of chivalric romance informed by adventure-time). Yet Gaudete's relationship to adventure-time as such is skewed and unstable, the narrative being shot through with a degree of spatial and temporal concretization that adventure-time by definition resists. Bakhtin describes what happens when the edge of 'everyday time' is introduced, as in the narrative of Gaudete, into the 'extratemporal hiatus' that is adventure-time:

> (. . .) the degree of *specificity* and *concreteness* of this world [adventure-time] is necessarily very limited. For any concretization — geographic, economic, sociopolitical, quotidian — would fetter the freedom and flexibility of the adventures and limit the absolute power of chance. Every concretization, of even the most simple and everyday variety, would introduce its own *rule-generating force*, its own *order*, its *inevitable ties* to human life and to the time specific to that life. Events would end up being interwoven with these rules, and to a greater or lesser extent would find themselves participating in this order, subject to its ties.

> This would critically limit the power of chance; the movement of the adventures would be organically localized and tied down in time and space.[22]

The protracted episode of the double's attempted escape at the end of the main narrative brings to a vacillating focus the oppressive and limiting force of quotidian reality on a 'hero' born in adventure-time: 'His fuel is burning too fast and smokily./ His knees tangle with their chemical limits' (p. 155). Inevitably the double is overwhelmed as the 'rule-generating force' of 'everyday' life takes its toll.

In *Gaudete*, then, adventure-time is dialogized against the edge of 'everyday time': the main narrative's setting within a single day, of which the reader is constantly reminded by the ominous emphasis placed on the sun's progress across the sky — 'And the sun crossing one more degree/ Bring the reaching of the landscape roots/ A fraction closer/ To the vicar's body' (p. 67) — foregrounds the claustrophobic pressure of everyday time and space on the changeling. Whereas the 'hammer of events' in strict adventure-time 'shatters nothing and forges nothing'[23], the collision of adventure-time and everyday time in *Gaudete* appears to shatter everything.

In this respect the book is more accurately placed in the tradition of what Bakhtin terms 'the *adventure novel of everyday life*'[24] (Bakhtin's key example is Apuleius's *The Golden Ass*): 'It is not the time of a Greek romance, a time that leaves no traces. On the contrary, it leaves a deep and irradicable mark on the man himself as well as on his entire life. It is, nevertheless, decidedly adventure-time: a time of exceptional and unusual events, events determined by chance, which, moreover, manifest themselves in fortuitous encounters (temporal junctures) and fortuitous nonencounters (temporal disjunctions)'[25]. While the mark left on the original Lumb by his ordeals is traced in the Epilogue poems, the end of the main narrative of *Gaudete* bears only the mark of catastrophic irresolution. As Bakhtin writes:

> Catastrophe is not finalization. It is the culmination, in collision and struggle, of points of view (of equally privileged consciousnesses, each with its own world). Catastrophe does not give these points of view resolution, but on the contrary reveals their incapability of resolution under earthly conditions; catastrophe sweeps them all away without having resolved them. Catastrophe is the opposite of triumph and apotheosis. By its very essence it is denied even elements of catharsis.[26]

At the end of the main narrative of *Gaudete*, 'All evidence goes up' (p. 170); Hughes speaks of 'the whole situation being impossibly crystallized in the immovable dead end forms of society and physical life'[27]. It is not until *Cave Birds* that Hughes attempts something like the imaginative reconciliation of the 'Two worlds' that in *Gaudete* circle each other 'Like two strange dogs' (p. 125).

As in *Gaudete*, in the 'adventure novel of everyday life' the initiatory role of chance is played down, the emphasis falling squarely on the hero's own moral accountability: 'He undoes the game of chance by his own prurience. The *primary initiative*, therefore, belongs to *the hero himself* and to his own *personality*. It is true that this initiative is *not positive in a creative sense* (but this is not very important); what we have is *guilt, moral weakness, error* (and in its Christian hagiographic variant, sin) as initiating forces'[28]. Lumb's failure to actively assist the ailing animal–woman in the Prologue seems to play a crucial role in kick-starting the overall 'adventure', yet why this should be so is by no means clear: the reader is forced to speculate as to the nature of Lumb's 'guilt' here. Lumb repeats a cultural and religious distinction — the Western binary opposition: spiritual/physical — that seems both to ordain and absolve his passivity: 'He is not a doctor. He can only pray' (p. 15). At this point Lumb is flogged unconscious and the elemental spirits set to work on producing Lumb's double from a log, as if Lumb here had inadvertently shot the albatross and set in motion an inscrutable chain of events that, as in Coleridge's poem, seems to have little to do with Christian conceptions of guilt and sin. For Hughes, the mysterious female figures in Coleridge's 'demonic' poems symbolize an 'elemental, thaumaturgic energy' that resides 'on the far side of his Christian Self's busy ratiocinations'[29], an energy that (on Hughes's reading) Coleridge's Christian conscience found difficult to come to terms with. On these terms, it is Lumb's own binaristic ratiocination that wrenches body and soul apart, the irresistible course of events it triggers off being at bottom a spontaneous psychosomatic reaction on the vicar's part, a reaction which to the 'unprepared' can, according to Hughes, be 'chaotic, terrifying, seemingly pathological'[30], and which by its very nature resists 'ratiocination' (much as the narrative itself resists interpretative explication).

THE DOUBLE'S DEFEAT

As mentioned, Hughes speaks of 'the whole situation being impossibly crystallized in the immovable dead end forms of society and physical life'. As the changeling flees across country towards the end of the main narrative, it is these 'dead end forms' that close on him and under which he is finally extinguished. Encoded in the dialogized intersection of everyday time and adventure-time here is a struggle between bodily and unconscious drives (coded as adventure-time) and their regulation by social law (coded as everyday time), of which the double and the men of the village are respective functions. Moments of overt adventure-time in the passage articulate the changeling's desire to outstrip the limit-imposing contingencies of mundane, 'normal' existence:

> He runs imagining
> Mountains of golden spirit, he springs across their crests.
> He has plugged his energy appeal into the inexhaustible earth.
> He rides in the air behind his shoulders with a whip of hard will
> Like a charioteer.
> He imagines he is effortless Adam, before weariness entered, leaping for God.
>
> (p. 163)

The hyperbolic language brought to a climax here a few lines later suffers collision with a flat, exhausted tone and phrasing that registers a different yet simultaneous 'time':

> At the same time
> He runs badly hurt, his blood inadequate,
> Hurling his limbs anyhow
> Lumpen and leaden, and there is no more air.
>
> (pp. 163–164)

What traps the double here is less social law than the very laws of physical life with which his own 'log-like' nature is, supposedly, co-extensive. The double seems less filled with elemental spirit life here and more a function of beset consciousness. In this sense the passage appears to register a kind of cross-over, focusing on the conscious thoughts and strategies of the duplicate vicar rather than on his erstwhile function as an agent of social disruption.

Hughes outlines the 'muddled' process by which the double becomes caught up in the social and cultural trappings of consciousness: 'going about its mission almost somnambulist, almost unconscious, tinkering with Heath-Robinson paper-back magical operations as an instinctive but muddled attempt to re-establish contact with the real origins and the real calling'. The double's 'log-like' attempts to inscribe himself within the terms of village life — to give his existence, or 'mission', meaning — are both grotesque and absurd, suggesting an impasse between social forms (Heath-Robinson paper-backs) and bodily life. The double's sudden nostalgia for 'ordinary human life' (after the debacle at the W.I. meeting he suddenly wishes 'Everybody back into their clothes and their discretion' [p. 150]) and his attempted escape at the end of the main narrative seem to suggest the inevitable entanglement of instinctual drives in the social order — in the prohibitions and taboos that constitute and support sociality: 'Then shouts catch and trip him, eyes have gripped him' (p. 159). By the same token, in so far as the double is literally losing spirit at this point and yearning for something like the original vicar's 'ordinary' consciousness to resume control, he is suddenly at odds with his own physical reality: 'His knees tangle with their chemical limits'.

THE LANGUAGE OF *GAUDETE*

The thematic contest in the main narrative between the social order (the men of the village) and that which eludes sociality (the double) is, as mentioned, played out in the very language of the narrative, which veers between overwrought metaphors and conceits — 'He imagines he is effortless Adam . . . leaping for God' — and a kind of flat monotone — 'He runs badly hurt . . . and there is no more air'. Given also the generic disjunction at the heart of the main narrative (adventure-time/realism), Terry Eagleton's linking of the language of *Gaudete* to 'traditional realism' requires some attention. Eagleton writes that 'one never has the feeling (. . .) that Hughes's language self-reflectively takes the measure of its own limits and capabilities; it is, rather, a language somehow locked tight in the bursting fullness of its presence, and so ironically closer to traditional realism than it would superficially seem'[31]. 'Bursting fullness' is perhaps a better description of Hughes's language than Eagleton intends, in that the language of the narrative is at times so full of itself that it seems to 'burst' its referential confines, its tangled metaphoricity and intertextuality in effect foregrounding its figurative status. Take the following line from the main narrative: 'The willows convulse, they coil and uncoil, silvery, like swans trying to take off' (p. 25). Deflected along a metaphorical loop and swamped by its own physicality, the line seems to want to writhe out of its referential shackles: by the time the image of the swan is registered, an image detonated by the coiling imagery and mimetic syntax, it is easy to forget that the denoted object here is trees; the language seems to shimmer: as the metaphorical vehicle (swans) overrides the tenor (willows), something of the transparency of the description is lost — a transparency on which traditional realism relies. The long lines of *Gaudete* detonate metaphor after metaphor in this way, the 'bursting fullness' of the language testifying to an ontological lack over which it makes its sound and fury. Taking full measure of its status as makeshift signification, Hughes's language articulates only what it projects: 'reality' as such in *Gaudete*, as the language strives to suggest, is an effect of consciousness; outside the perspectives of the characters it assumes at best a fleeting, uncertain status.

THE GROTESQUE IN *GAUDETE*

According to Eagleton, the language of *Gaudete* is 'insufficiently *inflected* and *articulated*', it lacks 'any "doubling" or genuine interplay of writing forms' and thus 'fails to assume any *attitude* to what it speaks of; it is positioned laconically outside those events, "mirroring" rather than constructing'[32]. I have already remarked on the interplay of generic forms in the main narrative of *Gaudete* (adventure-time/realism). As in *Crow*, the 'attitude' that the language of *Gaudete* adopts towards what it articulates is bound up with the book's immersion in what Bakhtin calls 'grotesque realism':

> Her brain swoons a little, trying to disengage. The glistening tissues, the sweating gasping life of division and multiplication, the shoving baby urgency of cells. All her pores want to weep. She is gripped by the weird pathos of biochemistry, the hot silken frailties, the giant, gristled power, the archaic sea-fruit inside her, which her girdle bites into, which begins to make her suit too tight.

> (p. 39)

If *Gaudete* is written against the backdrop of 'traditional realism' (as the book's unabashed use of stereotypes indicates), it uses this tradition as a dialogizing background, much as Old Testament Christianity in *Crow* forms the dialogizing background to Crow's Tricksterish or cartoon-like attempts to improvise a self. In the above passage, the transparent language of realism finds itself splintered by a 'grotesque' interplay of discordant registers — the languages of popular romance ('swoons a little', 'want to weep'), 'biochemistry' ('tissues', 'division and multiplication', 'cells', 'pores'), popular horror fiction ('the giant, gristled power') and an almost self-parodic tendency to exaggerate ('the archaic sea-fruit') all impinge on and collapse into one another — rendering the passage less a clear and cohesively framed 'mirror' onto reality than a hazy, shifting mosaic of incongruous images and diction.

Bakhtin writes that 'Contrary to modern canons, the grotesque body is not separated from the rest of the world. It is not a closed, completed unit; it is unfinished, outgrows itself, transgresses its own limits'[33]. Transgressing its own *discursive* limits, the language of *Gaudete* articulates something of the (grotesque) indeterminacy and fluidity of bodily life, a life that precedes and outflanks conscious (monologic) processing and co-ordination. It is into this primary world that the reader's perceptual stance is thrown in *Gaudete* — a world in which 'Lumb sees the lake is boiling' (p. 81) before the image may be reconstituted, by the reader, as rainfall on water.

THE EPILOGUE POEMS AND THE 'FUTURE ANTERIOR'

The first line of the first Epilogue poem — 'What will you make of half a man' (p. 176) — sounds a yearning, anticipatory note that is to mark the sequence as a whole: 'When you touch his grains, who shall stay?' (p. 178); 'How far can I fall?' (p. 180); 'So how will you gather me?' (p. 187); 'Let your home/ Be my home' (p. 190). The future-oriented thrust of the poems rings of the same 'task of completing the [socialized] "self" and [instinctual] "rhythm" dialectic' that Kristeva finds in Russian futurist poetry (Kristeva discusses Mayakovsky and Khlebnikov in these terms):

> But the irruption of semiotic rhythm within the signifying system of language (. . .) will not truly be experienced in the present. The rigid, imperious, immediate present kills, puts aside, and fritters away the poem. Thus, the irruption within the order of language of the anteriority of language evokes a later time, that is, a forever. The poem's time frame is some 'future anterior' that will never take place, never come about as such, but only as an upheaval of present place and meaning.[34]

'Semiotic rhythm' is Kristeva's term for the infantile drives and voicings that precede and underlie language acquisition, drives and voicings that return as rhythm and musicality in language, and especially in poetic language, which is the form of language use that gives most lease to rhythm and music. A more extensive discussion of Kristeva's theory of semiotic 'irruption' in language is to be found in the next chapter; it suffices to note here that, for Kristeva, our earliest, pre-linguistic experience — 'the anteriority of language' — cannot be grasped in words (if it is the case that we think only within the terms of language, then this seems an obvious explanation for why we cannot remember our earliest *pre-language* experiences), and that this land of oblivion tends to be unconsciously projected into Utopian, mythical or mystical visions of the future (Kristeva reads the Russian futurists in this light), a future that, in so far as this time of (retrospectively imagined) indivision or completeness has already been lost, can never come about.

For Kristeva then, semiotic rhythm is the 'drive or emotional force' in subjective utterance 'which does not signify as such but which remains latent in the phonic invocation or in the gesture of writing': 'This holds as much for more modest writings as for those called risqué, where the expression (more often that in texts by men) falls short of the emotional charge which gives rise to it'[35]. The 'rhythm' side of the instinctual rhythm/socialized self dialectic Kristeva identifies in Futurist poetry is in the Epilogue poems of

Gaudete constituted for the most part by the kind of expressive reticence Kristeva outlines above: it were as if 'semiotic' rhythm made its presence felt in these poems by being held in check, the terse, economic language and topographical sparsity of the poems expressing by falling short of the 'emotional charge' underlying them.

Neil Roberts points out that the unwritten half of *Gaudete*, mentioned by Hughes in letters and interviews and referred to in the Argument (the spirits want Lumb 'for some work in their world'), is in a sense embodied in the Epilogue poems, whose apostrophe form replaces the linear, sequential narrative with 'a discourse that is interior and timeless':

> Hughes's phrase 'the unwritten half of *Gaudete*' is deceptive. Certainly the narrative, brilliant as it is, can tell only half the story, but the Epilogue insinuates that the other half is not a 'story' at all. Whether Hughes realised it or not, the other half of *Gaudete* is not 'unwritten'. What is unwritten and unconscious as narrative is written and conscious as lyric. *Gaudete* might be seen as a work in which Hughes vindicates the genre which concedes least to the secular and bleak irreversibility of 'empirical time'.[36]

For Roberts, 'the fact that narrative has been supplanted by lyric is exactly what we have to understand'[37]: the adoption of the genre — the lyric apostrophe — 'which concedes least to the secular and bleak irreversibility of "empirical time"' in this sense obviously befits the articulation of spiritual or 'timeless' experience. Following Kristeva and Lacan, the spiritual/mystical experience the poems articulate can be theoretically located in a time before time and space as such are constituted, in the 'timelessness' or 'forever' of the pre-mirror stage infant, 'still sunk in his motor incapacity and nursling dependence'[38]. Again following Kristeva, it is the 'irruption' of such pre-linguistic experience in linguistic consciousness that gives rise to the mystical/religious experience of a 'forever', never to be realized in the here and now. Temporality — the time of 'realist' narrative — 'kills, puts aside, and fritters away' such experience. As Roberts points out, the lyrics of *Gaudete* (ostensibly spoken by Lumb, though there is no discernible distance between speaker and poet here) resist 'attenuation' of the deity: the goddess here is 'ambivalently present' in the very form of the poems, held in place by 'the urgency and intimacy of the address'[39].

Barthes finds this type of 'ambivalent presence' typical of 'Any episode of language which stages the absence of the loved object' (the idealized, unattainable nature of the female figure to whom the poems are addressed loosely recalls the courtly conventions of the Renaissance sonnet — the lover-poet's supplication to his Lady/muse): 'Endlessly I sustain the discourse of the beloved's absence; actually a preposterous situation; the other is absent as referent, present as allocutory. This singular distortion generates a kind of insupportable present; I am wedged between two tenses, that of the reference and that of the allocution: you have gone (which I lament), you are here (since I am addressing you). Whereupon I know what the present, that difficult tense, is: a pure portion of anxiety'[40]. In Lumb's lyrics, the goddess is 'absent as referent, present as allocutory': the apostrophe form of the poems allows the poet to sustain this ambivalent position and to bespeak the ordeal of a consciousness in the grip of the raptures and anxieties of a cry that, as one poem puts it, 'will not chill into syntax' (p. 176).

Thematically, then, the poems figure the dialectic between the self and its pre-linguistic ('semiotic') experience as a rupture between a 'nameless female deity' (Argument [p. 9]) — the namelessness of this deity suggests her pre-linguistic origins — and the poems' speaker, Lumb. Kristeva notes how Mayakovsky and Khlebnikov's 'leaps into mythology came from a nonexistent place in the future'[41]; similarly, Hughes's sublimation of what in psychoanalytical terms is the pre-Oedipal mother as an apocalyptic nature goddess provides the mythical support to negotiate an order of experience (Kristeva's 'future anterior') that defies language and sociality.

The language of the poems, in making anticipatory tracts across this implicit rupture in the self, is forced into a series of taut, oxymoronic twists and turns:

> How will you correct
> The veteran of negatives
> And the survivor of cease?
>
> (p. 176)

The elliptical, gnomic feel of the poems is in effect the index of a primordial object that has been irretrievably lost and yet continues to govern desire (desire as 'the survivor of cease' — the lost pre-Oedipal mother). The use of the apostrophe form in this sense constitutes an outcry against *absence*, speaking an impossible desire to fuse with the lost, archaic object: 'I know/ The flowers also look for you, and die looking' (p. 194).

The very words available to the poems' speaker betoken the lack-ridden nature of the self:

> Words buckle the voice in tighter, closer
> Under the midriff
> Till the cry rots, and speech
>
> Is a fistula
>
> Eking and deferring
>
> (p. 176)

Caught up in and deflected along the lacunary network of signs, the unconscious's search for its lost object finds itself infinitely 'deferred'. The poem announces explicitly the distrust of language implicit in the pared-down, elliptical, declarative language of the sequence, which gives the impression, as Hughes writes of Pilinszky's language, of words having 'escaped, only with great effort, from an intensifying, fixed core of silence'[42] (Hughes helped translate Pilinszky's *Selected Poems*, which were published in 1976, a year before the publication of *Gaudete*). It were as if the desire for 'oneness' with the deity as the means to self-completion necessitated a vigilant awareness of the 'Eking and deferring' tendencies of language, which as a result may only be used sparingly, as if to arrest the process of deferral.

Keith Sagar writes of the way in which the poems seem 'to throw images like ropes across the abyss between being and non-being'[43]. Their pared-down language certainly suggests a rope-like tautness:

> The coffin, spurred by its screws,
> Took a wrong turning.
>
> The earth can't balance its load
> Even to start.
>
> The creaking heavens
> Will never get there.

(p. 189)

The coffin here recalls the 'lifeboat-coffin' of 'Stations'; again it is the 'colloquial prose-readiness' of the poem's language — 'Took a wrong turning', 'can't balance its load', 'Will never get there' — that galvanizes the poem: in characteristic Hughes style, the poem seems to shift along a fault line between word and thing, a fault line materialized by the use of overtly clichéd, colloquial turns of phrase which sound incongruous, out of place, 'creaky'; the language of the poem itself never quite 'gets there'. Here this kind of ramshackle 'prose-readiness' is sharply curbed, the words of the poem uttered sparingly, as if under duress. It is upon the tautness achieved by this technique that the resonances of the more successful poems depend. However, not all the Epilogue poems achieve the striking tautness of phrasing of the above poem. The 'images like ropes' of some poems seem to fall slack, the simple, economic style merely curtailing Hughes's characteristic 'prose-readiness'. Again discussing Pilinszky, Hughes finds in the 'direct, simple, even "impoverished" ' properties of his language 'a marvel of luminosity, unerring balance, sinuous music and intensity — a metal resembling nothing else'[44]. The influence of Pilinszky and other East European poets (Hughes mentions Zbigniew Herbert, Miroslav Holub and Vasko Popa in the same essay) can be felt in the expressive reticence of the Epilogue poems, yet many of these poems lack the 'luminosity' Hughes finds in his East European exemplars, their stark, declarative language remaining at worst simply 'impoverished'.

NOTES

1. Ted Hughes, unpublished letter to Neil Roberts and Terry Gifford, October 1978.
2. Ekbert Faas, 'Ted Hughes and *Gaudete*', Interview with Ted Hughes, in Faas, *Ted Hughes: The Unaccommodated Universe* (Santa Barbara: Black Sparrow, 1980), p. 214.
3. Mikhail Bakhtin, *Problems of Dostoevsky's Poetics* ed. and trans. Caryl Emerson (Manchester: Manchester UP, 1984), p. 18.
4. I am indebted to Neil Roberts for pointing out these instances.
5. Faas, p. 214.
6. Terry Gifford and Neil Roberts, *Ted Hughes: A Critical Study* (London: Faber, 1981), p. 197.
7. *Ibid.*, p. 170.
8. A more detailed account of Lacan's notion of the trauma as a portion of the Real is to be found in chapter five in relation to Hughes's later poetry.
9. Neil Roberts, 'Hughes, Narrative and Lyric: An Analysis of *Gaudete*', in Keith Sagar (ed.), *The Challenge of Ted Hughes* (Basingstoke: Macmillan, 1994), p. 57.
10. Faas, p. 215.
11. Craig Robinson, *Ted Hughes as Shepherd of Being* (Basingstoke: Macmillan, 1989), p. 82.
12. Ted Hughes, *Winter Pollen: Occasional Prose* ed. William Scammell (London: Faber, 1994), p. 231.
13. Faas, p. 215.
14. Hughes, unpublished letter to Roberts and Gifford.
15. Jacques Lacan, *The Seminar of Jacques Lacan Book II. The Ego in Freud's Theory and in the Technique of Psychoanalysis 1954–1955* ed. Jacques-Alain Miller, trans. Sylvana Tomaselli (Cambridge: Cambridge University Press, 1988), p. 96.
16. Bakhtin, *Problems of Dostoevsky's Poetics*, p. 101.
17. *Ibid.*, p. 102.
18. I am indebted to Neil Roberts for pointing out that the rapid narrative events of *Gaudete* take place in a kind of dream-time.
19. Mikhail Bakhtin, *The Dialogic Imagination: Four Essays by M. M. Bakhtin* ed. Michael Holquist, trans. Caryl Emerson and Michael Holquist (Austin: University of Texas Press, 1981), p. 91.
20. *Ibid.*, p. 95.
21. *Ibid.*, p. 95.
22. *Ibid.*, p. 100.
23. *Ibid.*, p. 107.
24. *Ibid.*, p. 111.
25. *Ibid.*, p. 116.
26. Bakhtin, *Problems of Dostoevsky's Poetics*, p. 298.
27. Faas, p. 215.
28. Bakhtin, *The Dialogic Imagination*, pp. 116–117.
29. Hughes, *Winter Pollen*, pp. 461, 463.
30. *Ibid.*, p. 462.
31. Terry Eagleton, Review of *Gaudete*, in *Stand*, vol. 19 no. 2, 1978, p. 78.
32. *Ibid.*, pp. 78, 79.

33. Mikhail Bakhtin, *Rabelais and his World* trans. Hélène Iswolsky (Cambridge, Mass.: MIT Press, 1968), p. 26.
34. Julia Kristeva, *Desire in Language: A Semiotic Approach to Literature and Art* ed. Leon S. Roudiez, trans. Thomas Gora, Alice Jardine and Leon S. Roudiez (Oxford: Blackwell, 1981), p. 32.
35. Julia Kristeva, 'Talking about *Polylogue*', in Toril Moi (ed.), *French Feminist Thought: A Reader* (Oxford: Blackwell, 1987), p. 113.
36. Roberts, p. 69.
37. *Ibid.*, p. 66.
38. Jacques Lacan, *Écrits: A Selection* trans. Alan Sheridan (London: Tavistock/ Routledge, 1977), p. 2.
39. Roberts, p. 68.
40. Roland Barthes, *A Lover's Discourse: Fragments* trans. Richard Howard (London: Penguin, 1990), pp. 13, 14.
41. Kristeva, *Desire in Language*, p. 33.
42. Hughes, *Winter Pollen*, p. 231.
43. Keith Sagar, *The Art of Ted Hughes* second edition (Cambridge: Cambridge University Press, 1978), p. 224.
44. Hughes, *Winter Pollen*, p. 229.

CHAPTER FOUR

Cave Birds

A TRANSFORMATION MYSTERY

Given the notion of an often violently split, decentred self implicit in Hughes's early poetry and materialized in the figures of Crow and Lumb, it is significant that what appears to be the poet's imaginative attempt to heal and 'individuate' this self along a Jungian pathway[1] should prove to be his most obscure and difficult work. After the carnivalistic negativity of *Crow* and the catastrophic denouement of the main narrative of *Gaudete*, *Cave Birds: An Alchemical Cave Drama* (1978) draws on alchemical, mythological and shamanistic symbols and paradigms in order to project as mystical goal the Jungian ideal of the complete, integrated Self. According to Jung: 'Natural man is not a "self" — he is the mass and a particle in the mass, collective to such a degree that he is not even sure of his own ego. That is why since time immemorial he has needed the transformation mysteries to turn him into something, and to rescue him from the animal collective psyche, which is nothing but a *variété*. (. . .) Only a unified personality can experience life, not that personality which is split up into partial aspects, that bundle of odds and ends which also calls itself "man" '[2]. If *Crow* articulates carnivalistic *variété* (or, according to Freudian theory, the heterogeneous drives), then *Cave Birds* is Hughes's 'transformation mystery' in which the 'odds and ends' of potential selfhood are transfigured into an imaginative totality.

That this totality emerges from a sequence of highly stylized poems in the form of a bird suggests its problematic if not ironic status: neither 'The owl flower' nor 'The risen', poems in which the main dramatic threads and symbols of the book are drawn together and transmuted, admit for their subject any overtly human attributes, a quirk reflected in Baskin's accompanying drawings. In this light, the 'alchemical' of 'alchemical cave drama' suggests not only a Jungian paradigm of individuation but also something of the quack nature of the whole procedure, situated as it is in an imaginative 'cave' removed from ordinary reality. As with the slightly tongue-in-cheek Argument of *Gaudete*, the title of Hughes's and Baskin's book petitions a certain indulgence on the reader's part — we are to indulge the poet and artist their conceits. This kind of self-consciousness is evident in some of the more overtly quaint-florid, medieval-romance titles of the poems: 'First, the doubtful charts of skin', 'A flayed crow in the hall of judgement', 'As I came, I saw a wood', 'Bride and groom lie hidden for three days'. The wit of the best poems, which are invariably responses to Baskin's accompanying sketches, carries this same playful/self-conscious inflection, as in 'The interrogator':

> After, a dripping bagful of evidence
> Under her humped robe,
>
> She sweeps back, a spread-fingered Efreet,
> Into the courts of the after-life.

The Gothic, 'B'-movie imagery, accentuated on the page-spread by Baskin's appropriately 'humped' vulture, adds a touch of melodrama to the imaginative 'trial', foregrounding the status of the poem's conceit *as a conceit*. In both their sense of ready improvisation and esoteric reach, Hughes's conceits loosely recall those of the metaphysical poets of the seventeenth century. As with a poet like Donne, Hughes's conceits carry with them a rough and ready, spur-of-the-moment quality that demands we attend to the performance of wit and imagination on which the poem rides. When esoteric or mythological symbols are taken onboard by this kind of machinery they become subject to the same sense of provisionality that marks Hughes's work as a whole: all is gathered into the sweep of restless invention, nothing is allowed to settle into certainty.

LACAN AND JUNG

It is enough to turn to Lacan's caustic remarks on Jung to locate the reasons for Hughes's highly self-conscious handling of Jungian ideas in *Cave Birds*. Evoking the Jungian concept of the unconscious as 'find[ing] its lineaments in protomorphic proliferations of the image, in vegetative intumescences, in animic halos irradiating from the palpitations of life', Lacan writes:

> The whole difference between Freud's orientation and that of the Jungian school, which attaches itself to such forms, is there: *Wandlungen der libido* [Jung's book *Symbols of Transformation* (1912)]. These forms may be promoted to the first level of a mantic, for they can be produced by the appropriate techniques (promoting imaginary creations: reveries, drawings, etc.) in a mappable site (. . .) that is, in the veil of the narcissistic mirage, eminently suited to sustaining with its effects of seduction and capture whatever is reflected in it.
>
> If Freud rejected this mantic, it is at the point at which it neglected the directing function of a signifying articulation, which takes effect from its internal law and from a material subjected to the poverty that is essential to it.[3]

By situating the Jungian 'archetypal image' in 'the veil of the narcissistic mirage', Lacan empties it of any endogenous or self-sufficient significance; in this light, Hughes's and Baskin's imaginative bird–beings appear less as emanations of a postulated 'collective unconscious'[4] than as self–conscious projections, projections which implicitly comment on the ego's persistence in seeing its own form (albeit here in distorted fashion, mirroring a dis-integrating ego) reflected everywhere: Baskin's birds have anthropoid features, while in Hughes's poems these figures *speak*. This is all very much along the Jungian line of personifying and entering into dialogue with whatever dream forms the unconscious might throw up; it also forms a structural link with the 'dialogized' (in Bakhtin's sense) terrain of *Crow* and *Gaudete*, the uncertain, shifting use of personal pronouns in the poems — the 'contrapuntal roles played by birds and humans'[5] — effectively decentring the traditional 'monologic' centrality of the lyric 'I':

> When I said: 'Civilization,'
> He began to chop off his fingers and mourn.
> When I said: 'Sanity and again Sanity and above all Sanity,'
> He disembowelled himself with a cross shaped cut.
>
> 'After the first fright'

On the Jungian technique of improvising a dialogue with 'archetypal' figures encountered in dreams, Demaris Wehr writes: 'The ego sheds its usual harshness and its monolithic perspective and thus is transformed as well as relativized when it engages in "dialogue" with archetypal images such as the shadow, anima, or animus'[6]. While cutting through and relativizing an ego that aspires to be identical with itself, these acts of personification and dialogue are nevertheless Imaginary and Symbolic acts

— in Lacan's words they form a 'signifying articulation' — and as such achieve no direct purchase on any 'primordial' or 'instinctual' life outside these registers.

Significantly enough, the dramatic development of *Cave Birds* — the protagonist's confrontation by his 'shadow'[7] ('Shadow stark on the wall, all night long,/ From the street-light' — 'The summoner'; 'Small hope now for the stare-boned mule of man/ Lumped on the badlands, at his concrete shadow' — 'The interrogator'; 'This is your moon of pain — and the wise night-bird/ Your smile's shadow' — 'The plaintiff') from which appears the 'anima'[8] (the metamorphosing feminine bird-being of 'The interrogator', 'She seemed so considerate', 'The plaintiff', 'In these fading moments I wanted to say', 'A riddle', 'Bride and groom' etc.), leading up to and through a (Jungian/alchemical/shamanistic) process of death ('The executioner'), decomposition ('The knight') and resurrection ('The owl flower', 'The risen') — seems to make explicit use of Jungian ideas only to crucially diverge from Jung at the last minute: 'The risen' swerves clear of the Jungian goal of the 'unified personality' by implying the impossible *inhumanity* of such a position:

In the wind-fondled crucible of his splendour
The dirt becomes God.

But when will he land
On a man's wrist.

The falcon depicted here recalls the omnipotent hawk of 'The Hawk in the Rain', a bird that hangs 'Steady as a hallucination' over the floundering I-speaker of the earlier poem: both poems suggest that for the human subject the example of the bird of prey's God-like self-sufficiency can function only as a 'narcissistic mirage'.

It is in this movement toward a hypothetical Self that would negotiate and eventually extinguish or transcend the site of otherness in the self (the shadow/the anima) that Lacan locates the breaking point of the Jungian hypothesis: 'For if [the Other] is taken away, man can no longer even sustain himself in the position of Narcissus. As if by elastic, the *anima* springs back on to the *animus* and the *animus* on to the animal, which (. . .) sustains with its *Umwelt* [environment] "external relations" noticeably closer than ours, (. . .)'[9]. For Lacan, human experience depends on the otherness of language and social forms for its shape and meaning. In other words, without the other in the Lacanian sense, we would not be able to *reflect* on ourselves ('the position of Narcissus'), as we need something to reflect *with* or *against* (we ask: what was it/he/she *like*?). As 'The risen' implies, only the animal approximates the kind of unified selfhood that the human subject can only aspire to.

Looking to enter into dialogue with and assimilate the Jungian shadow and anima, the *Cave Birds* poems at every turn come up against the materiality of their own medium, the *otherness* of language. In the poem 'In these fading moments I wanted to say', the protagonist's anima is first described as 'murmuring', a word that onomatopoeically suggests a sub-verbal, unconscious origin to the utterance that is to displace the protagonist's exaggerated protestations; what is significant here is the function the colon serves between the anima's indirectly reported murmur and 'her' directly reported speech:

> But she was murmuring: Right from the start, my life
> Has been a cold business of mountains and their snow
> Of rivers and their mud
> Yes there were always smiles and one will do a lot
> To be near one's friends

The banal phrasing here ('one will do a lot') breaks the expectation of incoherence that 'murmuring' sets up. The colon after 'murmuring' in effect provides a concrete representation of what Lacan calls 'the language-barrier opposed to speech'[10]: as soon as the anima's murmur is translated into language then 'she' is necessarily inserted into an exogenous and pre-existing Symbolic order; the 'primordial' voice as such is lost, what is said in the poem is said on the surface of language.

That the protagonist's overstatements are displaced only by an*other* language (mannered, urbane) indicates the 'fading' the poem's title refers to to be the same 'fading' that for Lacan characterizes human subjectivity: 'All that is language is lent from this otherness and this is why the subject is always a fading thing that runs under the chain of signifiers'[11] (hence Lacan's parody of Descartes: 'I think where I am not, therefore I am where I do not think'[12]). Hughes's poem points up this fading through syntactic deferral and through the fading quality of the sound patterning, the clustered fricatives threatening to let the utterance through the 'language-barrier' into a drift of non-sense, the self through into non-being (the loss of all narcissistic 'reflection'):

> But after the bye-byes, and even before the door closed, even while the
>   lips still moved
> The scree had not ceased to slip and trickle
> The snow-melt was cutting deeper
> Through its anaesthetic
> The brown bulging swirls, where the snowflakes vanished into
>   themselves
> Had lost every reflection.

The syntax itself here 'slips and trickles' under the pressure of its own rhythm and musicality, a pressure that Kristeva terms the 'semiotic'.

THE SEMIOTIC AND THE SYMBOLIC

Kristeva's conception of the 'signifying process' — and in particular of the processes involved in 'poetic language' — as proposed in *Revolution in Poetic Language* (1979) holds further potential for demystifying Jung's elusive concepts and for laying bare the appeal of these concepts for the poet. Kristeva conceives of the 'semiotic' and (following Lacan) the 'symbolic' as the two sides of the signifying process. The semiotic involves pre-Oedipal drives that in the infant 'connect and orient the body to the mother'[13]: 'Discrete quantities of energy move through the body of the subject who is not yet constituted as such and, in the course of his development, they are arranged according to the various constraints imposed on this body (. . .) by family and social structures. In this way the drives, which are "energy" charges as well as "psychical" marks, articulate what we call a *chora*: a non-expressive totality formed by the drives and their stases in a motility that is as full of movement as it is regulated. (. . .) the *chora* precedes and underlies figuration and thus specularization, and is analogous only to vocal or kinetic rhythm'[14]. The semiotic *chora* is split at what Kristeva terms 'the *thetic* phase', a phase which is for Kristeva 'the threshold of language'[15] (in a sense embodied by the colon in 'In these fading moments'). Kristeva locates this phase in infancy as being initiated at the Lacanian 'mirror stage', the point where the infant, as a result of its perception of itself as in a mirror, perceives itself as separate from the mother and is thereby able to designate an 'other'. The mirror stage thus 'permit[s] the constitution of objects detached from the semiotic *chora*'[16]. This process of splitting and differentiation is the basis on which the infant enters language — the Symbolic order. On the subject's entry into the Symbolic order the semiotic *chora* 'acquires a more precise status', being manifest 'as a "second" return of instinctual functioning within the symbolic, as a negativity introduced into the symbolic order and as the transgression of that order'[17]. Transgressions of conventional language use in the form of breaks, ellipses, contradictions, repetitions, absences, illogical constructions and so forth are therefore directly traceable to the disruptive pressure of the semiotic within the Symbolic. Finally, 'Because the subject is always *both* semiotic *and* symbolic, no signifying system he produces can be either "exclusively" semiotic or "exclusively" symbolic, and is instead necessarily marked by an indebtedness to both'.[18]

In her later writing, Kristeva proposes a possible link between the idea of the semiotic and the Symbolic and the different regions and functions of the brain:

Cave Birds

Interruptions in linguistic sequentiality and even more so their
replacement with suprasegmental operations (rhythms, melodies) in
depressive discourse can be interpreted as deficiencies in the left
hemisphere, which controls linguistic generation, leading to domination
— temporary as it may be — by the right hemisphere, which controls
affects and emotions as well as their 'primary,' 'musical,' non-linguistic
inscriptions. (. . .) If one grants that language, within its own register,
must also translate that 'fluctuating state,' it follows that one must locate,
in language functioning, those levels that seem closer to the 'neuronal
brain' (such as grammatical and logical sequentiality) and those that
seem closer to the 'glandular brain' (the supra-segmental components
of discourse). One might thus be able to think out the 'symbolic
disposition' of significance in relation to the left hemisphere and the
neuronal brain, and the 'semiotic disposition' in relation to the right
hemisphere and the glandular brain.[19]

This position is in fact very close to Hughes's own remark on the relation-
ship between language and cerebral functioning:

The deeper into language one goes, the less visual/conceptual its
imagery, and the more audial/visceral/muscular its system of tensions.
This accords with the biological fact that the visual nerves connect with
the modern human brain, while the audial nerves connect with the
cerebellum, the primal animal brain and nervous system, direct. In other
words, the deeper into language one goes, the more dominated it
becomes by purely musical modes, and the more dramatic it becomes —
the more unified with total states of being and with the expressiveness of
physical action.[20]

The above comment appears in Hughes's notes on *Orghast*, a project Hughes
undertook with the theatre director Peter Brook and the International
Centre for Theatre Research. *Orghast* was the name of the play performed
by Brook's company of international actors at Persepolis, Iran, in 1971,
and of the language that Hughes invented for the play. The invented lan-
guage was based on instinctual sounds: in Kristevan terms, what Hughes
was aiming for here was a purely 'semiotic' language, a language of 'vocal
or kinetic rhythm', stripped of its figurative or conceptual function. Hughes's
description of the evolution of this language of pure instinctual sound is
interesting:

The drift of [Brook's] whole experiment at that time was to search for
a kind of theatre, or rather a kind of acting, which would communicate
to all human beings in that it wouldn't have the divisiveness of being
characterized by a single culture or a single language. (. . .) And to
begin with we had no language at all. We were just using bird-cries.
We were hoping to force the actors back into resources behind verbal
expressiveness, back into some sort of musical or other kind of
expressiveness. (. . .) So I just invented about half-a-dozen words and

automatically — because you don't want to invent meaningless sounds — I made each syllable represent what I considered to be one of the central ideas of the drama. I found from that that you could develop quite a large vocabulary, making different combinations of the root-syllables, and eventually I did develop an enormous vocabulary. Then automatically I began to introduce a grammar: I began to introduce cases, tenses — the whole thing just automatically turned into a language. And it wasn't as though I were thinking it out with great labour; it just automatically evolved in that way — on the pattern, I suppose, of Latin and so on, though it felt like instinct. But as it became a language, it began to work less and less well with the actors because, as it became more like an ordinary language, they began too to consider it as an ordinary language, they began to use it as a language in the scenes, so, instead of driving them right back into the absolute last-ditch efforts to express something or other that couldn't be expressed in words, they were simply talking, just using my language as ordinary language.[21]

According to Kristeva, the semiotic *chora* 'precedes and underlies figuration': Hughes here seems less to have broken through to a 'purely musical' mode of expression or communication than to the beginnings or underside of language, its instinctual lining. In other words, what Hughes seems to have discovered here is the impossibility of a purely instinctual language of sound — as soon as the instinctual sounds here are used to 'represent' an idea they 'automatically' turn into something like ordinary language (cases, tenses etc.). Hughes goes on in the same interview: 'To get [the actors] to reveal themselves again, we had to destroy that language and give them again a sequence of cries which had no verbal meaning. Then once again they were forced back onto other resources and tremendous, exciting, strange, musical things could happen again'[22]. It were as if purely musical expression were sustainable only at the cost of 'verbal meaning'. The risks here are obvious — as Hughes himself remarks: 'you don't want to invent meaningless sounds'.

It is in Hughes's poetry that the expressive resources of instinctual sound and rhythm — Kristeva's semiotic *chora* — are more successfully negotiated. As discussed in chapter one, Hughes's heavy emphasis on the audial and muscular side of language in early poems such as 'The Hawk in the Rain' and 'The Jaguar' — the pummelling stress patterns and bold use of alliteration, assonance etc. — has by *Wodwo* been played down, as if the expressive resources of sound and rhythm have run up against some kind of impasse: what Lacan calls the 'poverty' essential to language — its representational status, the word as a 'presence made of absence'. *Crow* sees Hughes adopt a 'super-simple and super-ugly' language, as if to point up this poverty, as well as its alienating effects. It is as if in Hughes's experiments in the early 1970s with an invented language of sound for the *Orghast* project and with a 'super-ugly' language in *Crow*, emptied of affect,

Hughes is exploring the twin aspects of language itself as defined by Kristeva — the semiotic and the Symbolic. Only the notes from the *Orghast* project survive (although the play was performed), and Hughes has never returned to what the subtitle of *Crow* — *From the Life and Songs of the Crow* — suggests is an unfinished or incomplete cycle of poems. Instead, Hughes has outstripped both positions — the meaningless sounds of *Orghast*, the empty language of *Crow* — by shifting emphasis onto the nature of the *relation* of music to meaning, of the semiotic to the Symbolic. It is something about the nature of this relationship that is figured — consciously or unconsciously — in *Cave Birds*.

THE HERMETIC VESSEL AS SEMIOTIC *CHORA*

The alchemists for Jung are of psychological interest in so far as they were 'chasing a projection, and that the more they attributed to the substance the further away they were getting from the psychological source of their expectations'[23]. Similarly, Kristeva writes that the nineteenth-century French poet Nerval's 'reference to the alchemical metamorphosis may be read as a metaphor more in keeping with the borderline experience of the psyche struggling against dark asymbolism than with a para-scientific description of physical or chemical reality'[24]. References to the alchemists' Hermetic vessel in *Cave Birds* — the 'cauldron of tongues' of 'The owl flower' and the 'wind-fondled crucible' of 'The risen' — are clearly to be read along these lines; still, the question remains as to what constitutes the *ground* of the alchemical metaphor in *Cave Birds*. Jung writes:

> For the alchemists the vessel is something truly marvellous: a *vas mirabile*. Maria Prophetissa says that the whole secret lies in knowing about the Hermetic vessel: 'Unum est vas' (the vessel is one) is emphasized again and again. (. . .) It is a kind of matrix or uterus from which the *filius philosophorum*, the miraculous stone, is to be born. (. . .) One naturally thinks of this vessel as a sort of retort or flask; but one soon learns that this is an inadequate conception since the vessel is more a mystical idea, a true symbol like all the central ideas of alchemy.[25]

In describing the Hermetic vessel as a 'mystical idea' or 'symbol' Jung practically occludes what he seeks to throw light on: nothing is revealed about the psychical space or process that the vessel in fact symbolizes[26]. This 'mystical idea', figured in *Cave Birds* by the image of a cauldron or crucible in which the protagonist is cast into in order to be pulverized and re-modelled, bears marked similarities to the Kristevan postulate of the semiotic *chora*, described by Kristeva as 'no more than the place where the subject is both generated and negated, the place where his unity succumbs before the process of charges and stases that produce him'[27]. This analogy would explain the uterine nature of the vessel, 'symbolic' as it is of a psychical space oriented around the maternal body. Hence also the dictum 'the vessel is one', enigmatically recalling the state of undifferentiated symbiosis experienced (according to psychoanalytical theory) by the pre-mirror stage infant (the 'not yet constituted' subject) with regard to the Mother.

The poem 'The executioner' squares up rhetorically to the threat of annihilation posed by the pre-verbal *chora* to the speaking being. The rhetorical form of the poem acts as Symbolic check or protection against the incantatory rhythm it simultaneously generates, a semiotic rhythm that for Kristeva aims ultimately to 'de-syn-thesize' the thetic phase ('He fills up the mirror' — 'The executioner'): 'In the extreme, negativity aims to foreclose the thetic phase, which, after a period of explosive semiotic motility, may result in the loss of the symbolic function, as seen in schizophrenia. "Art", on the other hand, by definition, does not relinquish the thetic even while pulverizing it through the negativity of transgression. Indeed, this is the only means of transgressing the thetic, and the difficulty of maintaining the symbolic function under the assault of negativity indicates the risk that textual practice represents for the subject'[28]. Jung also finds this psychical space fraught with risk: 'We must not underestimate the devastating effect of getting lost in the chaos, even if we know that it is the *sine qua non* of any regeneration of the spirit and the personality'[29]. Baskin's accompanying drawing to 'The executioner' threatens to blot out the page, the black shape seeming to be rendered manageable by its being conceived *symbolically* as a raven. The same tension holds for Hughes's poem: inverting the biblical account of creation, 'The executioner' maintains a Symbolic position that gestures towards its own collapse while simultaneously checking this collapse. The similes that seem arbitrarily tagged on at the end of lines 9 and 10 — 'He fills up the rivers he fills up the roads, like tentacles/ He fills up the streams and the paths, like veins' — (just as the raven's head seems tagged on to the black shape on the facing page) highlight this tension: it is as if the poet here were attempting to stall by stepping back from the runaway rhythm of the lines, the dislocated feel of the similes suggesting a growing struggle to find any *likeness* for the experience the poem describes.

'The owl flower' pushes the semiotic 'assault' further, drawing together and conflating the various motifs of the book that had hitherto carried a variously refined (from poem to poem) but more or less stable signification (within each nodal poem), only to 'pulverize' these motifs by wrenching them out of any stable, one-to-one link with what is referred to: 'A mummy grain is cracking its smile/ In a cauldron of tongues'. The kind of 'explosive semiotic motility' that threatens to 'sweep away' the Symbolic position is at its most marked here (the poem is virtually incomprehensible outside its imaginative context in the sequence and without Baskin's accompanying drawing), the heavily suggestive images resonating as if uncontrollably, throwing semantic emphasis off the poem's own field of representation and across the page-spread onto Baskin's owl, an owl which, as Gifford and Roberts note, 'seems to be hurtling towards the looker from the depths of space'[30]. In its heated and disorientating imagery (suggesting a phoenix-like rebirth), the poem seems to suggest something of the as yet raw and uncooled processes of its own production:

> The egg-stone
> Bursts among broody petals —
>
> And a staggering thing
> Fired with rainbows, raw with cringing heat,
>
> Blinks at the source.

In its conflated revolution of the sequence's main symbols and images ('flowers', 'flames', 'cauldron', 'mummy'), the poem overtly dramatizes what Kristeva describes as the 'remodelling' of the Symbolic order through 'the influx of the semiotic': 'Though absolutely necessary, the thetic is not exclusive: the semiotic, which also precedes it, constantly tears it open, and this transgression brings about all the various transformations of the signifying practice that are called "creation"'[31].

Hughes's sequence implicitly posits the necessity of somehow navigating this psychical space that Kristeva terms the semiotic *chora* if the healing, teleological function that Jung ascribes to the unconscious is to be embraced:

> 'The baptist'
> Enfolds you
> In winding waters, a swathing balm
>
> A mummy bandaging
> Of all your body's puckering hurts
>
> In the circulation of sea.

The highly textured use of fricatives, nasal resonants and semi-vowels here conveys the impression of the words sliding or dissolving into each other, as if in a murmur, a dissolve interrupted only momentarily by the harsher consonants of 'puckering hurts': suspended between its painful bonds to life and a melancholic withdrawal from these bonds ('mummy' as both corpse and the infantile word for mother seems to imply a link between such melancholic withdrawal and the Freudian postulate of a 'death drive'), the subject 'on trial' in *Cave Birds* is closer to the Kristevan 'subject in process/ on trial'[32] than Lacan's forever alienated subject, a subject for whom the 'space' that 'supports' the unconscious holds 'no friendship'[33]. Kristeva writes: 'In returning, through the event of death, towards that which produces its break; in exporting semiotic motility across the border on which the symbolic is established, the artist sketches out a kind of second birth'[34]. Although Kristeva implies all poetic language to be in some degree galvanized by 'semiotic motility', *Cave Birds* is particularly amenable to such a reading in that it raises its own semiotic processes to the level of theme: the imaginative trial of the book overtly dramatizes 'the event of death' through which the artist gains access to the *chora*, space of creation and regeneration.

THE SHAMANIC EVENT

The 'event of death' that according to Kristeva facilitates poetic creativity is analogous to the 'fundamental poetic event' that Hughes finds at the heart of shamanistic practice, a practice that in turn informs the pattern of imaginative death, disintegration and resurrection mapped in *Cave Birds*. Kristeva's conception of 'the symbolism of magic' being 'based on language's capacity to store up the death drive by taking it out of the body'[35] draws directly on Lévi-Strauss's characterization of the shaman's function as providing a 'language' for the sick subject 'by means of which unexpressed, and otherwise inexpressible, psychic states can be immediately expressed'[36]. The esoterica of *Cave Birds* — Egyptian mythology, shamanistic, alchemical and Jungian symbols — are best understood as thematicizing the poet's 'shamanistic' attempt to improvise 'a reorganization, in a favourable direction' (Lévi-Strauss[37]) of an experience that in fact bears all the marks of depression.

THE DISCOURSE OF DEPRESSION

Cave Birds is perhaps nothing more than a working through of depression, characterized by Kristeva as 'an abyss of sorrow, a noncommunicable grief that at times, and often on a long-term basis, lays claim upon us to the extent of having us lose all interest in words, actions, and even life itself'[38]. As the subject of Hughes's sequence at one point puts it: 'Whether dead or unborn, I did not care' ('She seemed so considerate'). The concluding image of 'In these fading moments', magnifying as it does a fairly mundane experience to hopelessly universal proportions, r_veals the insuperability of the depressive withdrawal that 'lays claim' to the subject of *Cave Birds*:

> The whole earth
> Had turned in its bed
> To the wall.

The central images and symbols that are revolved and transmuted throughout the sequence in this sense do not finally reveal, mandala-fashion, the central presence of the Jungian Self; rather they reflect what Kristeva calls the depressive's 'insistent' yet absent and unsignifiable 'Thing':

> The depressed narcissist mourns not an Object but the Thing. Let me posit the 'Thing' as the real that does not lend itself to signification, the center of attraction and repulsion, seat of the sexuality from which the object of desire will become separated.
>
> Of this Nerval provides a dazzling metaphor that suggests an insistence without presence, a light without representation: the Thing is an imagined sun, bright and black at the same time. 'It is a well-known fact that one never sees the sun in a dream, although one is often aware of some far brighter light.'[39]

The sun in *Cave Birds*, closely associated with Baskin's shadowy, black bird-forms, is similarly 'bright and black at the same time':

> This bird is the sun's key-hole.
> The sun spies through her.
>
> 'The interrogator'

> 'The executioner'
> Fills up
> Sun, moon, stars, he fills them up
> With his hemlock —
> They darken
>
> 'The executioner'

In this sense the self-consciously overwrought conceits and diction that mark the poems testify only to the finally ineffable nature of the depressed subject's 'Thing', described by Kristeva thus:

> Ever since that archaic attachment the depressed person has the impression of having been deprived of an unnameable, supreme good, of something unrepresentable, that perhaps only devouring might represent, or an *invocation* might point out, but no word could signify.

> (...) This 'something' would be previous to the detectable 'object':
> the secret and unreachable horizon of our loves and desires, it assumes,
> for the imagination, the consistency of an archaic mother, which,
> however, no precise image manages to encompass. The untiring quest
> for mistresses or, on the religious level, the accumulation of feminine
> divinities or mother goddesses that Eastern and particularly Egyptian
> religions lavish on the 'subject,' points to the elusive nature of the *Thing*
> — necessarily lost so that this 'subject,' separated from the 'object,' might
> become a speaking being.[40]

The changeling's sexual exploits in *Gaudete* have in *Cave Birds* been sub-
limated into a confrontation with Egyptian feminine divinities — the vulture
of 'The interrogator' has been identified as Nekhabet, a vulture goddess[41],
or the nature goddess Isis[42], while 'A flayed crow' contains a reference to
Maat, goddess of justice: 'My soul skinned, and the soul-skin laid out/ A
mat for my judges'. A poem like 'The executioner' is by no means simply
an 'invocation' of this 'devouring' that re-'fills' the depressed, lack-ridden
subject with its lost 'Thing': it is at the same time a *representation* of the
depressed state, a Symbolic 'container' (alchemical vessel) in which this
state is worked out and sublimated; Kristeva: 'How can one approach the
place I have referred to? Sublimation is an attempt to do so: through
melody, rhythm, semantic polyvalency, the so-called poetic form, which
decomposes and recomposes signs, is the sole "container" seemingly able
to secure an uncertain but adequate hold over the Thing'[43]. Kristeva could
be summing up the main theme and technique of Hughes's and Baskin's
book when she describes poetic language as a 'subtle alchemy of signs' that
facilitates what is experienced as 'a psychic transformation of the speaking
being between the two limits of nonmeaning and meaning, Satan and God,
Fall and Resurrection'[44].

It is in this context that the poet's rallying of the sublimatory 'machinery
of religion' and Jungian symbolism[45] can be seen for what it is, that is, as
constituting a Symbolic battle against the 'black sun' of depression, the
alchemist's *nigredo* [46] (given concrete visual form in Baskin's accompany-
ing drawings to 'The interrogator' and 'The executioner'). Kristeva writes:
'(...) aesthetic and particularly literary creation, and also religious dis-
course in its imaginary, fictional essence, set forth a device whose prosodic
economy, interaction of characters, and implicit symbolism constitute a
very faithful semiological representation of the subject's battle with sym-
bolic collapse. Such a literary representation is not an *elaboration* in the sense
of "becoming aware" of the inter– and intrapsychic causes of moral suf-
fering; that is where it diverges from the psychoanalytic course, which aims
at dissolving this symptom. Nevertheless, the literary (and religious) repres-
entation possesses a real and imaginary effectiveness that comes closer to

catharsis that to elaboration; it is a therapeutic device used in all societies throughout the ages'[47]. *Cave Birds* is less an 'elaboration' (it does not 'psychoanalyse' the symptom it wrestles with) than a sublimatory 'catharsis'; in keeping depression on the Symbolic move it remodels the disintegrating bonds to the other (and thus to language) that mark depressive withdrawal:

> And everything had become so hideous
> My solemn friends sat twice as solemn
> My jokey friends joked and joked
>
>   'She seemed so considerate'

As if to suggest the loss of 'interest in words, actions, and even life itself' that depression brings with itself, the meaninglessly repetitive language here seems to have run dry of any affect or emotion; the tone is flat, indifferent, much like the language of *Crow*, to which *Cave Birds* in this sense is a rejoinder: Kristeva points to '*the signifier's failure* to insure a compensating way out of the states of withdrawal in which the [depressed] subject takes refuge'[48] (Baskin's accompanying bird here seems to have collapsed into itself).

The 'failure' of the signifier here — the poem in effect 'signifies' depression through the empty signifiers that are symptomatic of the condition — constitutes the obverse of the platitude-ridden language of 'The scream', the opening poem of the sequence:

> All day the hawk perfected its craftsmanship
> And even through the night the miracle persisted.
> Mountains lazed in their smoky camp.
> Worms in the ground were doing a good job.

As the platitudes are stretched to cosmic dimensions — 'I knew I rode the wheel of the galaxy' (the concluding image of 'In these fading moments' reveals the depressive underside to the subject's narcissistic complacency here) — their ability to bear meaning attenuates and is finally punctured by the 'scream'. According to Kristeva, 'Depression is the hidden face of Narcissus, the face that is to bear him away into death, but of which he is unaware while he admires himself in a mirage'[49]. Effecting this change of face in the opening poem, *Cave Birds* sets out to transform the 'black sun' that rends and threatens to engulf the narcissist's world by projecting (with the support of religious, alchemical, Jungian symbolism etc.) improvisory meanings onto it, in the same way that Baskin's drawings of the raven and vulture in particular look like roughly improvised attempts to give some sort of negotiable form to a shape that otherwise threatens to black out the page.

THE PROBLEM OF THE FEMININE

The subject's changing relationship with his enigmatic and metamorphic feminine counterpart in the sequence — 'she' is at first accusatory and threatening (in the guise of a vulture in 'The interrogator') but later more reassuring and helpful ('A riddle', 'Bride and groom') — petitions a conceptualization in Jungian terms as a negotiation of the anima, the unconscious, feminine side of man's nature which the subject of *Cave Birds* on this reading comes to recognize and symbolically wed in 'Bride and groom'. The problem with this kind of reading lies in Jung's designation of an unconscious space or mechanism — the anima — as feminine.

Jung's gender-specific archetype bears a significant resemblance to Kristeva's notion of the 'enigmatic and feminine' *chora*: both are unconscious and have a potentially 'creative function'[50], both constitute (in Jung's words, describing the anima) 'a psychic reality which conflicts strongly with the world of the father'[51] (the Lacanian 'Name-of-the-Father' is the agency which facilitates the infant's entry into the Symbolic order by barring access to the maternal body, instituting the lack that henceforth supports the signifier). However, Kristeva's use of the term 'feminine' to describe the semiotic *chora* refers not so much to gender, but to the *chora*'s formative link with the pre-Oedipal mother (gender for Kristeva is conceivable only within the Symbolic order — hence 'the very dichotomy man/woman as an opposition between two rival entities may be understood as belonging to *metaphysics*'[52]: for Kristeva, there is no *essentially* or *inherently* feminine part of the psyche). In this light, the feminine presence in *Cave Birds* can be read less as a universalist statement on man's relationship with a postulated feminine side of his being than as a highly self-conscious attempt by the poet to give some sort of provisional form and voice to primary processes that pre-date and threaten to overturn the gendered self.

This position is in fact not far from Jung's own distinction between the 'archetype' and the 'archetypal image'. Demaris Wehr writes:

> Ambiguity had reigned in Jung's treatment of the archetypal images,
> especially with regard to their universality, until the 1946 clarification.
> At that point Jung claimed universality only for the archetype, not
> the image, and made it clear that they were two different things. The
> archetype itself was merely a predisposition to form images: 'The
> archetype in itself is empty and purely formal, nothing but a *facultas
> praeformandi*, a possibility of representation which is given *a priori*'.[53]

The archetypal image, on the other hand, is an effect of this 'irrepresentable, unconscious, pre-existent form' being 'filled out with the material of conscious experience'[54]. The universalism of Jung's archetypes is thus on closer examination compromised, refracted as their images are through the particular cultural and historical matrix which the self is subject to. Thus, in so far as it constitutes a hypothetical space that precedes representation, the anima begins to sound even more like Kristeva's 'theoretical supposition' of the semiotic *chora* that ' "precedes" symbolization'[55].

However, Jung seems to confuse his own distinction between 'archetype' and 'archetypal image' when he postulates the 'feminine' nature of the anima: as an 'empty and purely formal' category, the archetype in itself cannot be gender-specific; it acquires a sex only when *represented* through culturally and historically determined notions of gender. Produced within this historico-cultural field, the term 'feminine' is only meaningful within it and has no *unmediated* link with any primary or 'archetypal' processes that pre-date the self's constitutive entry into it.

Hughes's portrayal of the anima as a kind of mouthpiece for the unconscious in *Cave Birds* is fraught with ambiguity. When the anima speaks in the poems, she does so in a banal and 'inadequate' language (as in 'In these fading moments'), or else she speaks the paradoxical language of riddles:

Who am I?
Just as you are my father
I am your bride.
      'A riddle'

That the anima in *Cave Birds* 'reasons' through a displaced or paradoxical language points to the difficulty inherent in trying to articulate through the terms and distinctions of language a psychical space and drives that are irreducible to such terms and distinctions.

The *Crow* poem 'Crow's Undersong' in this sense anticipates *Cave Birds*. As its title indicates, the poem is concerned with the underside of the 'super-ugly' language of the sequence, and by implication the underside of language itself. The poem figures this 'undersong' of language as feminine: 'She comes dumb she cannot manage words'. For Kristeva, the 'enigmatic and feminine' *chora* is 'a space underlying the written [that] is rhythmic, unfettered, irreducible to its intelligible verbal translation; it is musical, anterior to judgement'[56]. 'Crow's Undersong' ironically exploits the disparity between social inscriptions (judgements) of the feminine and the 'unfettered', pre-social space underlying the inscribed: 'She comes sluttish she cannot keep house'. The poem characterizes this space largely through a process of negation: 'she' is enigmatically that which she is *not* — or rather 'cannot' — and is finally analogous only to the sometimes fitful, sometimes undulating rhythm of the poem.

Robert Graves's *The White Goddess* is an important influence on Hughes's feminine divinities (the feminine figure of 'Crow's Undersong', the 'nameless female deity' of *Gaudete*, the Egyptian divinities/Jungian anima of *Cave Birds*, the goddess of Hughes's book on Shakespeare, *Shakespeare and the Goddess of Complete Being*). Graves writes of the goddess:

> Her names and titles are innumerable. In ghost stories she often figures as 'The White Lady', and in ancient religions, from the British Isles to the Caucasus, as the 'White Goddess'. I cannot think of any true poet from Homer onwards who has not independently recorded his experience of her. The test of a poet's vision, one might say, is the accuracy of his portrayal of the White Goddess and of the island over which she rules. The reason why the hairs stand on end, the eyes water, the throat is constricted, the skin crawls and a shiver runs down the spine when one writes or reads a true poem is that a true poem is necessarily an invocation of the White Goddess, or Muse, the Mother of All Living, the ancient power of fright and lust — the female spider or the queen-bee whose embrace is death. Housman offered a secondary test of true poetry: whether it matches a phrase of Keats's, 'everything that reminds me of her goes through me like a spear'. (. . .) Keats was writing under the shadow of death about his Muse, Fanny Brawne; and the 'spear that roars for blood' is the traditional weapon of the dark executioner and supplanter.[57]

This is the dark executioner and supplanter of the *Cave Birds* poems — 'Your heart's winged flower/ Come to supplant you' ('The plaintiff') — and the feminine presence who comes only as far as 'nipples', 'fingertips', 'the tips of hair' and 'the fringe of voice' in 'Crow's Undersong' ('The reason why the hairs stand on end, the eyes water, the throat is constricted . . .').

In *Shakespeare and the Goddess of Complete Being*, Hughes historicizes this timeless figure of Graves's:

> By nature the two sides [of the brain] presumably live in a kind of happy marriage. A noisily chattering society is supercharged with right-side participation: music, song, dance, colour, imagery — and a vernacular tending naturally to imagery and musicality.
>
> But, as history demonstrates, the onset of rationality institutes proceedings for a kind of divorce. The electroencephalograph tells the story. At a definite moment, rationality acquires prestige (according to some celebrated examples, this happens where the Goddess-destroying god begins to get the upper hand). Rational philosophy proceeds by swift or groping steps to objective science. That is by the way. What matters inside the head, evidently, is that under the new dispensation of rationality, words (and rationality itself) nurture their innate tendencies — to abstraction and logic — in formulations that are increasingly exclusive of all other factors (on the tacit ideal model of mathematical inevitability). This new language, it seems, is the terms of the divorce. In other words, while the verbal reformulations of life, in this new language, become increasingly dominant in all human transactions, they become increasingly exclusive of any contribution from the right side. The result is an automatic suppression of right-side activity. In some

enclaves (particularly familiar in Western Protestant society) where the cultural incentives promoting the rational tendencies of language are extreme, the activity of the right side can be discredited and suppressed almost to extinction. The consequences, apparently, go deeper than the atmosphere of general aridity and colourless monotony, which are the obvious, perhaps (for many) tolerable signs.[58]

According to Hughes, the 'definite moment' in English history when 'rationality acquires prestige' is the Reformation, when the 'goddess' — in the form of Catholicism — 'was being put down, finally and decisively, by a pragmatic, sceptical, moralizing, desacralizing spirit: (. . .) the spirit of the ascendant, Puritan God of the individual conscience, the Age of Reason cloaked in the Reformation'[59]. In so far as Shakespeare's poems and plays 'incarnated the chemistry of the whole process', the *Complete Works* are 'modern England's creation story, our sacred book, closer to us than the Bible'[60]. For Hughes, Western civilization is still undergoing the arid effects of this dissociation of sensibility, the divorce instituted in Shakespeare's time between (Puritan) rationality and the (Catholic) 'goddess' — the 'mother tongue of the body'[61].

In charting the repressed world of the *chora* — the 'mother tongue of the body' — *Cave Birds* uncovers the price paid by the self for its constitutive entry into a culture 'where the (. . .) incentives promoting the rational tendencies of language are extreme': 'As your speech sharpened/ My silence widened' ('A riddle'). Poems like 'A riddle' and the uncollected *Cave Birds* poem 'Your Mother's Bones Wanted to Speak, They Could Not' seek to articulate just such an acknowledgement of debt:

Under the doomsday light of your mother's bones
Your paltriest words, your fleetest imaginations

Move like chains
Like bullets

Like iron pens
Carving your signature in the papery flesh.[62]

The penal imagery of 'Your Mother's Bones' insinuates not only the violent repression done to the semiotic *chora* by the self's constitutive dependence on words, but also the possible historical consequences ('chains', 'bullets') of this movement in societies that foster linear, objective, rational thought at the expense of the brain's right-side participation in the world (an earlier version of 'The plaintiff' evidently contains references to Herod, Stalin and the death camps among other things[63]).

However, Hughes's sequence remains problematic in so far as it inscribes the repressed *chora* as feminine. While such an inscription indicates the formative and persisting influence of the pre-Oedipal mother on the psyche, Hughes by the same token comes close to Jung's position of projecting the ambiguous and irrational aspects of the anima onto women. Demaris Wehr writes: 'Jung mentioned men's inability to perceive women clearly because of their anima projections, yet his own discussions of anima confusingly intermingle anima and the psychology of women. As a result, out of Jung's depictions of the anima emerge two blurred agendas. He often states specifically that he is going to discuss the anima — an aspect of male psychology — and then launches into a discussion of the psychology of women'[64]. Similarly, in poems such as 'Something was happening', 'After there was nothing there was a woman' and 'Bride and groom' it is unclear whether Hughes is portraying women or the anima, and to what extent anyway the two are related.

Although in the poem 'Bride and groom' the mechanical way in which the two figures give shape to each other might suggest the socially constructed nature of gender — 'He oils the delicate cogs of her mouth/ She inlays with deep-cut *scrolls* the nape of his neck' (my italics) — the organic imagery of 'After there was nothing there was a woman' casts the feminine in an essentialist light:

> Whose breasts had come about
> By long toil of earthworms
> After many failures, but they were here now
> And she protected them with silk

The notion of the feminine as being close to if not continuous with the rhythms of nature plays straight into the hands of the type of damaging cultural stereotypes that Wehr charges Jung with 'naturalizing'[65].

NOTES

1. For a straightforward Jungian interpretation of *Cave Birds*, see Leonard M. Scigaj, *Ted Hughes* (Boston: G. K. Hall, 1991), pp. 101–108.
2. C. G. Jung, *Psychology and Alchemy* revised edition (London: Routledge, 1968), p. 81.
3. Jacques Lacan, *Écrits: A Selection* trans. Alan Sheridan (London: Tavistock/ Routledge, 1977), p. 195. It is against such conceptions of the unconscious as Jung's that Lacan's own pronouncements on the unconscious take on a striking and outspoken edge: 'The unconscious is neither primordial nor instinctual; what it knows about the elementary is no more than the elements of the signifier'; *ibid.*, p. 170.
4. Jung writes: 'The instincts and archetypes together form the *collective unconscious*. I call it "collective" because, unlike the personal unconscious, it is not

made up of individual and more or less unique contents but of those which are universal and of regular occurrence. (. . .) The deeper "layers" of the psyche lose their individual uniqueness as they retreat farther and farther into darkness. "Lower down," that is to say as they approach the autonomous functional systems, they become increasingly collective until they are universalised and extinguished in the body's materiality, i.e., in chemical substances. The body's carbon is simply carbon. Hence "at bottom" the psyche is simply "world"'; Glossary to C. G. Jung, *Memories, Dreams, Reflections* recorded and ed. Anelia Jaffé, trans. Richard and Clara Winston (London: Flamingo, 1983), p. 420.

5. Note to Ted Hughes, *Selected Poems 1957–1981* (London: Faber, 1982), p. 237.
6. Demaris S. Wehr, *Jung and Feminism: Liberating Archetypes* (London: Routledge, 1988), p. 58.
7. Jung writes: 'The shadow personifies everything that the subject refuses to acknowledge about himself and yet is always thrusting itself upon him directly or indirectly — for instance, inferior traits of character and other incompatible tendencies'; Glossary to *Memories, Dreams, Reflections*, p. 417.
8. Jung writes: 'Every man carries with him the eternal image of woman, not the image of this or that particular woman, but a definitive feminine image. This image is fundamentally unconscious, an hereditary factor of primordial origin engraved in the living organic system of the man, an imprint or "archetype" of all the ancestral experiences of the female, a deposit, as it were, of all the impressions ever made by women . . . Since this image is unconscious, it is always unconsciously projected upon the person of the beloved, and is one of the chief reasons for passionate attraction or aversion'; *ibid.*, p. 410.
9. Lacan, *Écrits*, p. 195.
10. *Ibid.*, p. 71.
11. Jacques Lacan, 'Of Structure as an Inmixing of an Otherness Prerequisite to Any Subject Whatever', in Richard Macksey and Eugenio Donato (ed.), *The Structuralist Controversy: The Languages of Criticism and the Sciences of Man* (London: Johns Hopkins University Press, 1970), p. 194.
12. Lacan, *Écrits*, p. 166.
13. Julia Kristeva, *The Kristeva Reader* ed. Toril Moi (Oxford: Blackwell, 1986), p. 95.
14. *Ibid.*, pp. 93, 94.
15. *Ibid.*, pp. 99–100.
16. *Ibid.*, p. 100.
17. *Ibid.*, p. 118.
18. *Ibid.*, p. 93.
19. Julia Kristeva, *Black Sun: Depression and Melancholia* trans. Leon S. Roudiez (New York: Columbia University Press, 1989), pp. 38, 39.
20. Note by Ted Hughes, in A. C. H. Smith, *Orghast at Persepolis* (London: Methuen, 1972), p. 45.
21. Clive Wilmer, Interview with Ted Hughes, *P. N. Review* vol. 19 no. 3, Jan-Feb 1993, p. 38.
22. *Ibid.*, p. 38.
23. Jung, *Psychology and Alchemy*, p. 146.
24. Kristeva, *Black Sun*, pp. 151–152.
25. Jung, *Psychology and Alchemy*, pp. 236–238.
26. According to Lacan, 'The Jungian investigation (. . .) intrigues by its quaintness, its style, the parallels it establishes between what some mental or religious

ascesis produces and what a schizophrenic produces. That, perhaps, is a way of working which has the advantage of adding some colour and life for the benefit of the researchers, but which quite clearly has illuminated nothing in the way of mechanisms (. . .)'; *The Seminar of Jacques Lacan Book 1. Freud's Papers on Technique 1953–1954* ed. Jacques-Alain Miller, trans. John Forrester (Cambridge: Cambridge University Press, 1988), p. 116.

27. Kristeva, *The Kristeva Reader*, p. 95.
28. *Ibid.*, p. 119.
29. Jung, *Psychology and Alchemy*, p. 74.
30. Terry Gifford and Neil Roberts, *Ted Hughes: A Critical Study* (London: Faber, 1981), p. 202.
31. Kristeva, *The Kristeva Reader*, p. 113.
32. According to Kristeva, 'poetic language puts the subject in process/on trial through a network of marks and semiotic facilitations'; *The Kristeva Reader*, p. 110.
33. Jacques Lacan, *The Four Fundamental Concepts of Psychoanalysis* ed. Jacques-Alain Miller, trans. Alan Sheridan (London: Penguin, 1977), p. vii.
34. Kristeva, *The Kristeva Reader*, p. 120.
35. *Ibid.*, p. 129.
36. Claude Lévi-Strauss, *Structural Anthropology* trans. Claire Jacobson and Brooke Grundfest Schoepf (London: Penguin, 1963), p. 21.
37. *Ibid.*, p. 21.
38. Kristeva, *Black Sun*, p. 3.
39. *Ibid.*, p. 13.
40. *Ibid.*, pp. 13, 145.
41. Craig Robinson, *Ted Hughes as Shepherd of Being* (Basingstoke: Macmillan, 1989), p. 113.
42. Stuart Hirschberg, *Myth in the Poetry of Ted Hughes* (Dublin: Wolfhound Press, 1981), p. 173.
43. Kristeva, *Black Sun*, p. 14.
44. *Ibid.*, p. 101.
45. Wehr writes of the way in which Jungian psychology itself functions as a religion: 'Analytical psychology (. . .) is also a symbol system. Although its symbols are not fixed or static theoretically, once they have been named and conceptualized, they tend to function as givens. The shadow, animus, anima, and self take on the functions previously ascribed to Jesus, the Virgin Mary, God, and the devil, becoming psychologized, "inner" versions of a religious symbol system'; *Jung and Feminism*, pp. 83–84.
46. Jung writes: 'The *nigredo* or blackness is the initial state, either present from the beginning as a quality of the *prima materia*, the chaos or *massa confusa*, or else produced by the separation (*solutio, separatio, divisio, putrefactio*) of the elements'; *Psychology and Alchemy*, p. 230. The alchemists' *nigredo* is analogous to the depressive's unsignifiable 'Thing' (Nerval's 'black sun') from which, according to Kristeva, 'the object of desire will become separated' (the alchemists' philosophical stone?).
47. Kristeva, *Black Sun*, p. 24.
48. *Ibid.*, p. 10.
49. *Ibid.*, p. 5.
50. Jung, *Psychology and Alchemy*, p. 177.
51. *Ibid.*, p. 73.

52. Kristeva, *The Kristeva Reader*, p. 209.

53. Wehr, *Jung and Feminism*, p. 51.

54. Jung, Glossary to *Memories, Dreams, Reflections*, p. 411.

55. Kristeva, *The Kristeva Reader*, p. 118.

56. *Ibid.*, p. 97.

57. Robert Graves, *The White Goddess: A Historical Grammar of Poetic Myth* amended edition (London: Faber, 1961), pp. 24–25.

58. Ted Hughes, *Shakespeare and the Goddess of Complete Being* (London: Faber, 1992), p. 157.

59. *Ibid.*, p. 85.

60. *Ibid.*, p. 85.

61. *Ibid.*, p. 160.

62. Ted Hughes, 'Your Mother's Bones Wanted to Speak, They Could Not', published in Keith Sagar (ed.), *The Achievement of Ted Hughes* (Manchester: Manchester University Press, 1983), p. 348.

63. Keith Sagar, *The Art of Ted Hughes* second edition (Cambridge: Cambridge University Press, 1978), p. 176.

64. Wehr, *Jung and Feminism*, p. 104.

65. Wehr writes: 'If feeling is the primary function of most women — which it is in the Jungian view — then thinking will be most women's inferior function. Therefore, when a woman thinks, it is likely to be in an "unadapted," unpracticed way. The problem with this kind of Jungian explanation (. . .) is that it gives a "natural" explanation for a behaviour that has been strongly conditioned by patriarchal standards'; *ibid.*, pp. 46–47.

CHAPTER FIVE

Later Hughes

THE REAL AS OBSTACLE

After the 'experimental' volumes of the 1970s (*Crow, Gaudete, Cave Birds*), *Moortown* (1979) can be seen to represent a transitional stage between these and Hughes's more accessible recent work: the comparatively short 'mythic' sequences of the book suggest Hughes's use of myth as a way of conceiving of a Real beyond the ken of consciousness to be near exhaustion; the poem 'No God — only wind on the flower', from the *Prometheus on his Crag* sequence, constitutes a kind of hole in the mythic frame that exposes the *provisional* status of this frame:

> No God — only wind on the flower.
> No chains — only sinews, nerves, bones.
> And no vulture — only a flame
> A word
> A bitten-out gobbet of sun
> Buried behind the navel, unutterable.
> The vital, immortal wound.
> One nuclear syllable, bleeding silence.

For all the poet's attempts to make metaphoric tracts into this 'unutterable' Real, to decipher possible meanings with the aid of myth, the Real nonetheless stays firmly and silently in place: 'Buried behind the navel'.

The flexible, open-ended style of the *Moortown* sequence (the poems were originally journal entries) seems to attest to the difficulty of finding any stable meaning in a world posited as indifferent to human concerns, a difficulty thematicized by focusing on Hughes's own experience of farming in Devon. Just as the farmer wrestles with and makes 'manageable'

'the world of half-ton hooves, and horns, / And hides heedless as cedar-
boarding' ('Hands'), so the poet tries to wrench some sort of meaning from
a world that resists human projections. In the poem 'Tractor' a frozen
tractor is 'an agony/ To think of'. In the poem the farmer's attempt to
start a frozen tractor is directly analogous to the poet's attempt to make
'tracts' into an obstinate Real with language. Lacan writes: 'The real is the
impact with the obstacle; it is the fact that things do not turn out all right
straight away, as the hand that is held out to external objects wishes'[1]. The
recalcitrance of the object provides the impetus for much of Hughes's
poetry. The technique is self-reflective: the poet can only make the experi-
ence with the object mean anything by personifyng it — in response to the
speaker's attempts to start it up the frozen tractor 'just coughs./ It ridicules
me'. In so far as the poem's speaker thinks, he meets only his own pro-
jections, his capacity for illusion. Yet despite the illusory, self-reflective
quality of the imagery here, there is something heroic about the whole
procedure: in being humanized life is made more manageable, as if it were
in this very process of imaginative projection (against the odds) of human
meaning (onto a void) that our humanity as such resided: the frozen tractor
of the poem finally comes to life, 'Raging and trembling and rejoicing';
man and machine have merged in a kind of primordial exultancy at over-
coming the intractable.

Metaphor is Hughes's basic tool for making improvisory tracts into the
Real as such. More often than not the metaphoricity of the process is
foregrounded, as in the following poem from *River* (1983):

Painful

To think of the river tonight — suffering itself.
I imagine a Caesarean,
The wound's hapless mouth, a vital loss
Under the taut mask, on the heaped bed.

The silent to-fro hurrying of nurses,
The bowed stillness of surgeons,
A trickling in the hush. The intent steel
Stitching the frothing womb, in its raw hole.

And walking in the morning in the blue glare of the ward
I shall feel in my head the anaesthetic,
The stiff gauze, the congealments.
'New Year'

The conceit — 'I imagine a Caesarean' — is developed to the extent that
it is easy to forget that this is a description of a river: as a possible meaning
here 'congeals' it acts like an 'anaesthetic', blocking out the intimation of
a dumb, gaping, 'raw' reality — 'The wound's hapless mouth . . . the frothing
womb, in its raw hole'. It is as if what is too 'painful' to imagine can

nevertheless be 'stitched up' with words, yet at the cost of covering over the original painful insight: 'I shall feel in my head the anaesthetic'.

The Real for Hughes is thus what human meaning covers over, what words veil; but it is also what may rend this veil (of language-based consciousness) at any moment. In the poem 'Where I Sit Writing My Letter', from *Flowers and Insects* (1986), the I-speaker is disturbed by a flock of starlings: 'And I'm just quieting thoughts towards my letter/ When they all come storming back'. Lacan writes of a rupture between perception and consciousness:

> The other day, I was awoken from a short nap by knocking at my door just before I actually awoke. With this impatient knocking I had already formed a dream, a dream that manifested to me something other than this knocking. And when I awake, it is in so far as I reconstitute my entire representation around this knocking — this perception — that I am aware of it. I know that I am there, at what time I went to sleep, and why I went to sleep. When the knocking occurs, not in my perception, but in my consciousness, it is because my consciousness reconstitutes itself around this representation — that I know that I am waking up, that I am *knocked up*.[2]

For Lacan, consciousness is an effect of a 'constituted and represented reality'[3], in relation to which the Real is 'this obstacle, this hitch, that we find at every moment'[4]. In this light the poem 'New Year' seems to show how consciousness reconstitutes itself— 'congeals' — against what disturbs it, while 'Where I Sit Writing My Letter' shows the same in reverse: 'I'm just quieting thoughts towards my letter' suggests the dependency of consciousness on language (the ability to *represent* experience), a consciousness which can thus only experience the Real as a disturbance — the speaker of the poem is left 'fevered, and addled' by the starlings. The 'Where next? Where now? Where?' of the starlings echoes the tractor of 'Tractor' 'Shouting Where Where?', signalling the openness of Hughes's later poetic, its receptivity to experiences that language is normally in danger of foreclosing.

THE REAL AS TRAUMA

Following Lacan, while the Real may be encountered 'at every moment' as a hitch or obstacle, it is in the form of the trauma that its presence is most keenly felt. It is in this same guise — 'that which is *unassimilable*'[5] — that the Real is most explicitly encountered in Hughes's later poetry:

My post-war father was so silent
He seemed to be listening. I eavesdropped
On the hot line. His lonely sittings
Mangled me, in secret — like TV
Watched too long, my nerves lasered.

'Dust As We Are' (from *Wolfwatching* [1989])

Hughes's father was one of only seventeen survivors of his regiment
that fought at Gallipoli. Hughes's first poems about the First World War
appear in his first volume, *The Hawk in the Rain* (1957). In the more recent
Wolfwatching Hughes is still trying to come to terms with this legacy: the
poems here, however, contain none of the charged language, careful shap-
ing and clear cut ironies of Hughes's earlier 'war' poems such as 'The
Casualty', 'Bayonet Charge', 'Griefs for Dead Soldiers' and 'Six Young
Men' (all from *The Hawk in the Rain*). 'Bayonet Charge' ends:

He plunged past with his bayonet toward the green hedge.
King, honour, human dignity, etcetera
Dropped like luxuries in a yelling alarm
To get out of that blue crackling air
His terror's touchy dynamite.

Compared with the charged sound patterns and rhythm here, the language
of the 'war' poems from *Wolfwatching* is flat, even clichéd:

Naked men
Slithered staring where their mothers and sisters
Would never have to meet their eyes, or see
Exactly how they sprawled and were trodden.

'Dust As We Are'

Whereas the tone of 'Bayonet Charge' is knowingly ironic, the tone here
is straightforward and *un*ironic. The word 'Exactly' is telling: it is as if the
poem's words were skirting what is unassimilable in the experience they
describe: words here can never be 'exactly' right. The use of a demonstrat-
ive in the last line of the poem bears this impression out (the words here
have more of an *indexing* function than a signifying one):

After mother's milk
This was the soul's food. A soap–smell spectre
Of the massacre of innocents. So the soul grew.
A strange thing, with rickets — a hyena.
No singing — that kind of laughter.

'*That* kind of laughter' — the appeal here is to a feeling that resists approx-
imation by words.

In a review of *Wolfwatching*, John Lucas writes: 'one can't help noticing the slack phrasing. It is as though the writer feels the material is sufficiently shocking to require no shaping'[6]. He quotes the following lines from the poem 'For the Duration' to demonstrate his point:

> Maybe you didn't want to frighten me.
> Now it's too late.
> Now I'd ask you shamelessly.
> But then I felt ashamed.
> What was my shame? Why couldn't I have borne
> To hear you telling what you underwent?

Lucas comments: 'Surely these are notes towards a poem rather than the poem itself?'[7]. The prosaic, notational style here is indeed reminiscent of the poems from the *Moortown* sequence, which began as journal entries. Yet to say that the *Moortown* poems and certain poems from *Wolfwatching* do not constitute 'poetry' as such would be to impose preconceived ideas about what a poem is — Lucas mentions Hughes's lack of 'shaping' in these poems — onto poems that seem indifferent to such preconceptions. The loose, prosaic structure of Hughes's later poetry in effect allows the Real to emerge as an obstacle or snag impossible to assimilate in any 'well-made poem' (Hughes has tried and abandoned the 'well-made poem' by the time his third volume, *Woduo*, appears).

Other criteria are needed if how Hughes's later poetry works is to be gauged; Lucas himself admits he is at a loss: 'Perhaps one has to admit, rather blankly, that when a Hughes poem works it works. The question of prosody somehow doesn't arise'[8]. In his own critical prose, Hughes himself points up what he is after:

> A strange quality of truth is that it is reluctant to use words. Like
> Cordelia, in *King Lear*. Perhaps the more sure of itself a truth is, the
> more doubtful it is of the adequacy of words. This struck me forcibly
> once when I was collecting material for what I hoped would be a long
> poem about the campaign on Gallipoli during the First World War.
> (. . .)
> I had an enlightening experience talking to two of the survivors —
> one eloquent, one taciturn, both unsophisticated serious men, and they
> talked about the war in general. The eloquent one had been badly
> wounded, the other one only slightly. Yet from the eloquent one I
> seemed to get very little, merely anecdotes. From his monosyllabic friend
> something so frightening and terrible came over, that even now I
> remember that man's memories with caution. Both had lived through
> and registered the same terrific events. Yet words and natural, narrative,
> dramatic skill concealed everything in the one. While in the other,
> exclamations, hesitating vague words, I don't know what, just something
> about his half movements and very dumbness released a world of
> shocking force and vividness.[9]

'For the Duration' goes on:

> Why was your war so much more unbearable
> Than anybody else's? As if nobody else
> Knew how to remember. After some uncle's
> Virtuoso tale of survival
> That made me marvel and laugh —
> I looked at your face, your cigarette
> Like a dial-finger. And my mind
> Stopped with numbness.
>
> Your day-silence was the coma
> Out of which your night-dreams rose shouting.

What these poems articulate is the difficulty faced by the poet in coming to terms with an experience that is traumatic in the Lacanian sense of being resistant to conscious assimilation: it is this slow struggle with what it is that lacerates language and consciousness, rather than any final resolution or 'shaping' of it, that the poems embody. The language has the looseness and open-endedness of prose; aware of its limitations, it self-consciously falls short of what it wants to say, generating an affective charge or remainder that is felt to be finally intractable — as if only a tentative, 'inadequate' language were able to register the actuality and truth of the matter.

THE PHOTOGRAPH AS REAL

As a preface to *Remains of Elmet* (1979), Hughes explains that it was Fay Godwin's photographs of the Calder valley that 'moved me to write the accompanying poems', implying a formative relationship between the photographs and poems similar to that between Leonard Baskin's drawings and Hughes's poems in *Cave Birds* (1978) (the relationship between Hughes's poems and Peter Keen's photographs in *River* [1983] seems more incidental). A good example is the poem 'The Big Animal Of Rock', which reads like a direct response to Godwin's accompanying photograph, which depicts a black outcrop of rock that seems to rear up out of the snow as if alive, as if reaching heavenwards. The poem takes as its starting point these aspects of the photograph:

> 'The Big Animal Of Rock'
> Is kneeling
> In the cemetery of its ancestors.

It is as if the occasion of the poem were to provide a language (here a religious register) for what Barthes in referring to the photograph calls 'the pressure of the unspeakable which wants to be spoken'[10]. According to Barthes, in so far as 'The photograph is literally an emanation of the referent'[11] it belongs to the Lacanian category of the Real:

> In the Photograph, the event is never transcended for the sake of something else: the Photograph always leads the corpus I need back to the body I see; it is the absolute Particular, the sovereign Contingency, matte and somehow stupid, the *This* (this photograph, and not Photography), in short, what Lacan calls the *Tuché*, the Occasion, the Encounter, the Real, in its indefatigable expression. In order to designate reality, Buddhism says *sunya*, the void; but better still: *tathata*, as Alan Watts has it, the fact of being this, of being thus, of being so; *tat* means *that* in Sanskrit and suggests the gesture of the child pointing his finger at something and saying: *that, there it is, lo!* but says nothing else; a photograph cannot be transformed (spoken) philosophically, it is wholly ballasted by the contingency of which it is the weightless, transparent envelope. (. . .)
>   A specific photograph, in effect, is never distinguished from its referent (from what it represents), or at least it is not *immediately* or *generally* distinguished from its referent (as is the case for every other image, encumbered — from the start, and because of its status — by the way in which the object is simulated): it is not impossible to perceive the photographic signifier (certain professionals do so), but it requires a secondary action of knowledge or of reflection. By nature, the Photograph (. . .) has something tautological about it: a pipe, here, is always and intractably a pipe.[12]

If anything Godwin's photographs exploit this peculiarity of the medium — its *asymbolic* status. As Barthes puts it: 'The effect is certain but unlocatable, it [the photograph] does not find its sign, its name; it is sharp yet lands in a vague zone of myself; it is acute yet muffled, it cries out in silence'[13]. That is, Godwin's bleak landscapes seem to 'cry out in silence' (as in the photograph that accompanies the poem 'The Big Animal Of Rock'), providing the occasion for the poems as self-conscious divinations of their possible meanings:

> The cantor
> The rock,
> Sings.
>   'The Big Animal Of Rock'

As pure 'contingency', what stares from Godwin's photographs is a pure, dumb Real that the 'encumbered' language of the poems (encumbered with social, religious and cultural meanings) can never aspire to, just as the photographs themselves necessarily remain 'undeveloped' as signs; Barthes writes:

'This brings the Photograph (certain photographs) close to the Haiku. For the notation of a haiku, too, is undevelopable: everything is given, without provoking the desire for or even the possibility of a rhetorical expansion'.[14] It is this latent, inverse tension between the two mediums — the photograph cannot speak, language has no purchase on the Real — that Godwin and Hughes manipulate to great effect, making the photographs and poems of the book all of a piece.

The tendency of Godwin's photographs to 'cry out in silence' is picked up thematically by Hughes — thus a tree:

> Under unending interrogation by wind
> Tortured by huge scaldings of light
> Tried to confess all but could not
> Bleed a word
>
> Stripped to its root letter, cruciform
> Contorted
> Tried to tell all
>
> Through crooking of elbows
> Twitching of finger-ends.
>
> Finally
> Resigned
> To be dumb.

'A Tree'

Against the suggestive glare of Godwin's photographs, Hughes is better able to develop a sense of the arbitrariness of signs, their noisy unreality: the language and imagery of the above poem suggest a kind of torturous inquisition, as if the very dumbness of the Real constituted the necessary underside and goad to the sound and fury of signs.

AN 'INTERNALLY PERSUASIVE DISCOURSE'

In an interview Hughes says: 'I grew up in West Yorkshire. They have a very distinctive dialect there. Whatever other speech you grow into, presumably your dialect stays alive in a sort of inner freedom, a separate little self. (. . .) Without it, I doubt if I would ever have written verse'[15]. While a kind of North Country directness is implicit in all Hughes's work, it is in *Remains of Elmet* — the meditative sequence about industrial decline around Hughes's childhood home — that Yorkshire dialect is used most explicitly: 'Days are chucked out at night . . . the slogging world' ('Lumb Chimneys'); 'They get by/ On the hill subsidy' ('The Sluttiest Sheep In England'); 'Shitty bony cattle disconsolate' ('Auction').

The direct, no–nonsense character of Yorkshire dialect Hughes finds rooted in social and historical contingencies: 'A poverty/ That cut rock lumps for words' ('For Billy Holt'). In invoking these contingencies *Remains of Elmet* explicitly interrogates the ideologies that inform Hughes's own consciousness. The sequence in effect enacts a kind of exorcism — a laying to rest of the ghost of history and a transformation or extenuation of what Bakhtin calls an 'internally persuasive discourse' (the dialect of Hughes's childhood home):

> Internally persuasive discourse — as opposed to one that is externally authoritative — is, as it is affirmed through assimilation, tightly interwoven with 'one's own word.' In the everyday rounds of our consciousness, the internally persuasive word is half–ours and half–someone else's. Its creativity and productiveness consist precisely in the fact that such a word awakens new and independent words, that it organizes masses of our words from within, and does not remain in an isolated and static condition. It is not so much interpreted by us as it is further, that is, freely, developed, applied to new material, new conditions; it enters into interanimating relationships with new contexts. (. . .) The semantic structure of an internally persuasive discourse is *not finite*, it is *open*; in each of the new contexts that dialogize it, this discourse is able to reveal ever newer *ways to mean*.[16]

This is similar to what Hughes says about the way dialect 'stays alive in a sort of inner freedom'. In *Remains of Elmet*, Hughes manipulates what Bakhtin calls the 'open' structure of an internally persuasive discourse (Yorkshire dialect) in order to make it mean something new; that is, the poems employ a language already saturated with ideological inflections, but compel this language to reverberate with *other* meanings. Thus the Protestant work ethic — 'Wesley's foundation stone' ('Mount Zion') — is denaturalized by being placed in an ahistorical context of organic growth, decay and renewal:

Days are chucked out at night.
The huge labour of leaf is simply thrown away.
Great yesterdays are left lying.

Nose upwind, the slogging world
Cannot look aside or backward.

'Lumb Chimneys'

And the sun climbed into its wet sack
For the day's work

'Cock-Crows'

According to Bakhtin, 'A few changes in orientation and the internally persuasive word easily becomes an object of representation'[17]. Hughes's reorientation of Yorkshire dialect and its ideological freighting within new contexts in effect objectifies this dialect — some of the poem titles seem in themselves to encapsulate the technique: 'Rock Has Not Learned', 'The Sluttiest Sheep In England'. Here the object of representation is less any rock or sheep than the very language and point of view they are seen from.

The poems of the sequence figure the historical and cultural forces that have shaped this 'common view', exploring the combined legacy of the Industrial Revolution — 'migraine of headscarves and clatter/ Of clog-irons and looms' ('The Trance of Light') — and decline — 'The towns and the villages were sacked' ('First, Mills'), Wesley's Methodism and the Protestant work ethic — 'And clog-irons and biblical texts' ('The Trance of Light'), and the First World War and its aftermath — 'The hills were commandeered/ For gravemounds' ('First, Mills'). The poems place this combined legacy against the backdrop of the Pennine landscape, which 'cries out in silence' in the photographs. The effect is Zen-like: language, history and culture seem to be shouldered off by the insistent '*this*-ness' of light, water, stone and sky: 'And the swift glooms of purple/ Are swabbing the human shape from the freed stones' ('Top Withens').

Its ideological baggage X-rayed and off-loaded, Hughes retains the direct, crude character of Yorkshire dialect to improvise self-conscious 'short cuts' into a Real that in the end remains indifferent to human meanings: 'blind skylines revolving dumbly// Ignorant in ignorant air' ('Rock Has Not Learned'). Hughes's comments on Shakespeare's language shed light on his own practice:

It wasn't a super-processed super-removed super-arcane language like Milton . . . it was super-crude. It was backyard improvisation. It was dialect taken to the limit. That was it . . . it was inspired dialect. The whole crush and cramming throwaway expressiveness of it was right at the heart of it dialect. So immediately I felt he was much closer to me than to all those scholars and commentators at the bottom of the page who I assumed hadn't grown up in some dialect. It enabled me to see all sorts of virtues in him. I saw all his knotted up complexities and piled up obscurities suddenly as nothing of the sort . . . they were just the result of his taking short cuts through walls and ceilings and floors. He goes direct from centre to centre but you never see him on the stairs or the corridors. It's a sort of inspired idleness. Wherever he turns his attention, his whole body rematerializes at that point. It's as if he were too idle to be anything but utterly direct, and utterly simple.[18]

Remains of Elmet is exactly this: 'dialect taken to the limit', where 'Something that was fingers and/ Slavery and religious' now 'reflects sky' ('Willow-Herb').

THE IMAGINARY-REAL

Hughes's anthropomorphic imagery would at first glance seem to belie the possibility of reflecting anything but the ego's Imaginary projections:

> Obsolete despair
> Smiles this toothless and senile
> Mauve-pink flower.
>
> 'Willow-Herb'

Yet Hughes's anthropomorphism is not straightforwardly narcissistic. Something of the inappropriateness of the conceit is registered here — it fails to take hold, two images are evoked and held in tension: an old, 'toothless and senile' man or woman and a 'mauve-pink flower'. In effect, the 'this-ness' of the flower is registered in so far as it eludes the poem's conceit.

On the relation of narcissism to the external world, Lacan writes:

> What did I try to get across with the mirror stage? That whatever in man is loosened up, fragmented, anarchic, establishes its relation to his perceptions on a plane with a completely original tension. The image of his body is the principle of every unity he perceives in objects. Now, he only perceives the unity of this specific image from the outside, and in an anticipated manner. Because of this double relation which he has with himself, all the objects of his world are always structured around the wandering shadow of his own ego. They will all have a fundamentally anthropomorphic character, even egomorphic we could say. Man's ideal unity, which is never attained as such and escapes him at every moment, is evoked at every moment in this perception. The object is never for him definitively the final object, except in exceptional circumstances. But it thus appears in the guise of an object from which man is irremediably separated, and which shows him the very figure of his dehiscence within the world — object which by essence destroys him, anxiety, which he cannot recapture, in which he will never truly be able to find reconciliation, his adhesion to the world, his perfect complementarity on the level of desire. It is in the nature of desire to be radically torn.[19]

The poem 'Daffodils', from *Flowers and Insects* (1986), begins by painting the flowers as a 'perfect complement' to the I-speaker's desire:

> I'd bought a patch of wild ground.
> In March it surprised me. Suddenly I saw what I owned.
> A cauldron of daffodils, boiling gently.
>
> A gilding of the Deeds — treasure trove!
> Daffodils just came. And kept coming —
>
> 'Blown foam,' I wrote, 'Vessels of light!'

The poem's title and its high spirited beginning, as well as the poetry *quoted* within the poem, seems to cast a glance at Wordsworth's daffodils, as does

the idea of the daffodils as 'treasure' or 'wealth' — 'I gazed — and gazed —
but little thought/ What wealth the show to me had brought' (Wordsworth,
'I Wandered Lonely as a Cloud'[20]) — although for the speaker of Hughes's
poem, this seems to be material wealth only: 'Suddenly I saw what I owned'.
'I wandered lonely as a cloud' becomes in Hughes's poem:

> I was still a nomad.
> My life was still a raid. The earth was booty.
> I knew I'd live forever.

The poem up until this point seems to dance carelessly along in something
like the spirit of Wordsworth's poem, but then suddenly slips into another
mood:

> I had not learned
> What a fleeting glance of the everlasting
> Daffodils are. Did not recognise
> The nuptial flight of the rarest ephemera —
> My own days!
> Hardly more body than a hallucination!

The anxiety intimated here — that the daffodils, and by extension the I-
speaker's 'own days', somehow constitute a 'hallucination' — is elaborated
later on in the poem:

> I tried to picture them out there — in the garden —
>
> These rigid, gold archangels somehow
> Drank up my attempt.
> They became awful,
> Like the idea of atoms. Or like the idea
> Of white-frosted galaxies, floating apart.

Stripped of their 'egomorphic' character — the flowers no longer comple-
ment the I-speaker's 'ideal unity' (thoughts such as: 'I knew I'd live forever')
— the daffodils reveal something anarchic. Lacan writes: 'does not the con-
ceptual area into which we thought we had reduced the real later refuse
to lend its support to physicist thinking?'[21]. This perception — the universe
as entropy, 'dehiscence' of the ego's 'ideal unity' — is latent in Wordsworth's
poem, where the daffodils are 'Continuous as the stars that shine/ And
twinkle on the milky way'; Hughes's poem picks up on and amplifies this
intimation.

Shouldering off the speaker's narcissistic projections, the daffodils are
now (following Lacan) an object which 'destroys', an object in which the
speaker finds no reflection. It is precisely this oscillation — the object as
Imaginary complement of desire, the object as intimation of an anxiety-
provoking Real — that Hughes's anthropomorphic imagery is structured

around. 'The Honey Bee', also from *Flowers and Insects*, tries to conceive of this *other* side of the object (beyond narcissism):

> The Honey Bee
> Brilliant as Einstein's idea
> Can't be taught a thing.
> Like the sun, she's on course forever.
>
> As if nothing else at all existed
> Except her flowers.
> No mountains, no cows, no beaches, no shops.
> Only the rainbow waves of her flowers
>
> A tremor in emptiness
>
> A flying carpet of flowers

Just as the honey bee cannot conceive of 'the conceptual area into which we thought we had reduced the real' — 'No mountains, no cows, no beaches, no shops' — so the beekeeper cannot imagine anything beyond this conceptual area (the beyond of physicist thinking, 'Einstein's idea'):

> Furry goblin midgets
> (The beekeeper's thoughts) clamber stickily
> Over the sun's face — gloves of shadow.

It is as if the poet's task were to get beyond 'the wandering shadow of his own ego', to imagine the unimaginable, which may be ecstatic as well as disturbing: the poem 'Go Fishing', from *River*, ends:

> Become translucent — one untangling drift
> Of water-mesh, and a weight of earth-taste light
> Mangled by wing-shadows
> Everything circling and flowing and hover-still
>
> Crawl out over roots, new and nameless
> Search for face, harden into limbs
>
> Let the world come back, like a white hospital
> Busy with urgency wards
>
> Try to speak and nearly succeed
> Heal into time and other people

Again the poem reads like a series of notes, as if anything more structured would necessarily foreclose the experience, which is essentially one of *loss*: 'Become translucent — one untangling drift . . . *nameless*'. The ego reconstitutes itself in relation to '*other*' people', to a conceptual world that by the end of the poem seems disturbing: 'like a white hospital/ Busy with urgency wards'.

At the extreme, when the weight of the social contract is no longer manageable (or has been shattered by trauma), the letter of this contract and the 'little reality' it supports are soluble — whether the affective solvent is a form of ecstasy ('Gnat-Psalm, 'Go Fishing') or sadness:

You would
Stop the needle and without a word
Begin to weep quietly. Like a singing.
With no other care, only to weep
Wholly, deeply, as if at last
You had arrived, as if now at last
You could rest, could relax utterly
Into a luxury of pure weeping —
Could dissolve yourself, me, everything
Into this relief of your strange music.

'Source' (from *Wolfwatching*)

What *Crow* articulates in its own blackly carnivalistic way has here been humanized, translated back into the terms of an instantly recognizable human experience.

However, the key note struck by Hughes's later body of poetry is high-spirited, so much so that Hughes in places seems to smile at his own excesses, the kind of special effects that have become his trademark. As a note to the poem 'Rain-Charm for the Duchy', from the collection of Laureate poems of that name (1992), Hughes writes: 'that drought of 1984 broke with a heavy storm':

The car-top hammered. The Cathedral jumped in and out
Of a heaven that had obviously caught fire
And couldn't be contained.
A girl in high heels, her handbag above her head,
Risked it across the square's lit metals.

It is moments like this — when a larger, 'uncontainable' reality breaks into our 'little reality' and changes everything — that Hughes is quick to seize on. The phenomenal world here has become a kaleidoscopic hallucination, as if this were somehow its Real nature. Lacan writes: 'In the end, doesn't the feeling of the real reach its high point in the pressing manifestation of an unreal, hallucinatory reality?'[22] The manifestation of this feeling, breaking up and transforming ordinary reality, is a hallmark of Hughes's later work.

NOTES

1. Jacques Lacan, *The Four Fundamental Concepts of Psychoanalysis* ed. Jacques-Alain Miller, trans. Alan Sheridan (London: Penguin, 1977), p. 167.

2. *Ibid.*, p. 56.
3. *Ibid.*, p. 60.
4. *Ibid.*, p. 54.
5. *Ibid.*, p. 55.
6. John Lucas, 'The exclusive eye', *TLS* October 20–26, 1989, p. 1148.
7. *Ibid.*, p. 1148.
8. *Ibid.*, p. 1148.
9. Ted Hughes, *Winter Pollen: Occasional Prose* ed. William Scammell (London: Faber, 1994), pp. 122–123.
10. Roland Barthes, *Camera Lucida: Reflections on Photography* trans. Richard Howard (London: Fontana, 1984), p. 19.
11. *Ibid.*, p. 80.
12. *Ibid.*, pp. 4–5.
13. *Ibid.*, pp. 52–53.
14. *Ibid.*, p. 49.
15. Ekbert Faas, 'Ted Hughes and *Crow*', Interview with Ted Hughes, *London Magazine* vol. 10 no. 10 January 1971, pp. 11–12.
16. Mikhail Bakhtin, *The Dialogic Imagination: Four Essays by M. M. Bakhtin* ed. Michael Holquist, trans. Caryl Emerson and Michael Holquist (Austin: University of Texas Press, 1981), pp. 345–346.
17. *Ibid.*, p. 347.
18. Faas, p. 13.
19. Jacques Lacan, *The Seminar of Jacques Lacan Book II. The Ego in Freud's Theory and in the Technique of Psychoanalysis 1954–1955* ed. Jacques-Alain Miller, trans. Sylvana Tomaselli (Cambridge: Cambridge UP, 1988), p. 166.
20. William Wordsworth, 'I Wandered Lonely as a Cloud', in Harold Bloom and Lionel Trilling (ed.), *Romantic Poetry and Prose* (Oxford: Oxford University Press, 1973), p. 174.
21. Jacques Lacan, *Écrits: A Selection* trans. Alan Sheridan (London: Tavistock/Routledge, 1977), p. 27.
22. Jacques Lacan, *The Seminar of Jacques Lacan Book I. Freud's Papers on Technique 1953–1954* ed. Jacques-Alain Miller, trans. John Forrester (Cambridge: Cambridge University Press, 1988), pp. 66–67.

CHAPTER SIX

Hughes as Laureate

In 1984 Hughes was appointed Poet Laureate. Given Hughes's reputation at the time as a poet who celebrates the amoral and often violent energies of nature — 'his insisting upon foxes and bulls and violence' (Seamus Heaney) — as pitted against the civilizing norms of society, and given the charges of 'nihilism' and 'sadism' levelled at *Crow* by some critics, the appointment might seem — and seemed to many at the time — incongruous. As Neil Roberts put it in a review of Hughes's first Laureate poem, 'Rain-Charm for the Duchy, A Blessed, Devout Drench for the Christening of His Royal Highness Prince Harry', thinking of Hughes as the Poet Laureate 'is like thinking of Emily Brontë as lady-in-waiting to Queen Victoria'[1]. Even critics and readers responsive to the mythical/religious strains in Hughes's poetry found the appointment incongruous: in the same review Roberts points out that the monarchy is a Christian institution, 'And those responsible for appointing the Laureate have chosen a poet who is pagan in the strongest possible sense, who has described the Christian God as "the man-created, broken-down, corrupt despot of a ramshackle religion"'[2]. Writing at the same time as Roberts (1985), Seamus Heaney saw the incongruity of Hughes's appointment as arising not so much from Hughes's 'paganism', but from the seemingly anachronistic nature of Hughes's 'essentially religious vision' in a modern, secularized society:

> Britain today is a country apparently obsessed with its fatigued class war and its self-wounding industrial crises, a country whose destiny is debated in terms of economics; whose official church is almost embarrassed by the mention of God; whose universities falter in their trust in the traditional humanist disciplines. That such a country should turn to a poet with an essentially religious vision, without a word to say on

contemporary politics but with a strong trust in the pre-industrial realities of the natural world, is remarkable. In fact, it is a vivid demonstration of the truth of the implied message of Hughes's poetry that the instinctual, intuitive side of man's, and in particular the Englishman's, nature has been starved and occluded and is in need of refreshment.[3]

Either way, both Heaney and Roberts saw the incongruities of Hughes's appointment as making it particularly apt: for Heaney, Hughes's first Laureate poem — a description of a downpour after a drought in the West country — re-established 'an aspect of one of the most ancient rites of Indo-European kingship, the betrothal of the King to his physical territory. By dedicating the poem to the young Prince Henry and by drenching the royal domain, the Duchy of Cornwall, in a shower of benediction, Hughes not only made a graceful gesture but reaffirmed an ancient tradition and re-established, without sanctimoniousness, a sacerdotal function for the poet in the realm'[4]. For Roberts, there is a certain irony at work in the poem — 'a lurking, goblin-like amusement at the disproportion between this drench and the wetting that the prince actually experienced in church': Hughes rejuvenates by subverting his new office, but in a 'convivial, warm and mannerly' way[5].

Yet it would be easy to be heavy-handed when using terms such as 'irony' or 'subversion' in relation to Hughes's role as Laureate. In the notes that Hughes provides to the collection of Laureate poems published in 1992 — *Rain-Charm for the Duchy and other Laureate Poems* — the poet speaks of his 'boyhood fanatic patriotism' (p. 53), while the volume as a whole is prefaced by the lines:

A Soul is a wheel.
A Nation's a Soul
With a Crown at the hub
To keep it whole

At first glance there does not seem to be much in the way of subversive irony here. What the notes and poems do do is to historicize and qualify the 'boyhood fanatic patriotism' Hughes speaks of: 'The British outlook that I describe here, I realize, is now almost entirely limited to those born after the First World War but before the late thirties — that slightly different species who took in the blood of the First World War with their mother's milk, and who up to their middle age knew Britain only as a country always at war, or inwardly expecting and preparing for war' (p. 59). Passages like this illuminate an important aspect not only of the Laureate poems, but of Hughes's poetry in general: what lends Hughes's poems their distinctive form of ambivalence, their ability to wrong-foot

and disturb the reader, is their sense of complicity with the energies —
natural, religious, historical — they interrogate. That is, there is a strong
sense in Hughes's poems that in order to exorcise a ghost it must be
allowed to speak, and Hughes's biggest ghost is the First World War and
the shock waves it sent through his family:

> Still spellbound by that oath at Agincourt,
> That palace jewel — the bullet Nelson bore.
> But Passchendaele and Somme disturb me more.
>
> Being British may be fact, faith, neither or both.
> I only know what ghosts breathe in my breath —
> The shiver of their battles my Shibboleth.
>
> 'A Masque for Three Voices, For the Ninetieth Birthday
> of Her Majesty Queen Elizabeth the Queen Mother'

Much as Hughes qualifies his 'patriotism' by delineating its historical
determinants, by finding the self to be continuous with — though never
reducible to — such determinants, so any notion of national or ethnic
purity that might cling to the word 'British' is undermined in the volume
by Hughes's sense of the history of the British Isles, which in Hughes's
vision have always been a kind of multi-cultural melting-pot, the British
people 'genetically the most mixed-up gallimaufry of mongrels on earth'
(p. 63).

While the prefatory lines to Hughes's volume of Laureate poems seem
(in the words of one reviewer) to leave 'no room for disloyalties'[6], the
collection as a whole gives a sense of the uneasiness and precariousness of
the parts that currently make up the 'whole'. Of the need for some kind
of workable unifying vision, symbolized by the Crown, Hughes is in no
doubt — though this vision itself can only ever be improvisory and pro-
visional, to be continually re-negotiated: 'a melt of strange metals./ To be
folded and hammered,/ Re-folded, re-hammered' ('A Birthday Masque,
For Her Majesty Queen Elizabeth II's Sixtieth Birthday'). In the context
of the current climate of uncertainty about the role of the monarchy in a
secular democracy, and given the increasingly isolated standing in a multi-
cultural society of the Queen as head of the Church of England, there is
surely a message here from the Laureate to his Queen. As Hughes writes
in a note to the above poem: 'This term, "the ring of the people", occurs
in the memoir by the great Sioux Shaman Black Elk, who saw "the ring"
of his people "broken" in a prophetic vision of the disintegration of the
Sioux nation as an independent moral unity. Yet his visionary concept of
"the ring of the people" embraced, finally, all the different peoples of the
earth, not only his own tribesmen' (p. 55).

NOTES

1. Neil Roberts, 'Ted Hughes and the Laureateship', *Critical Quarterly* vol. 27 no. 2, summer 1985, p. 3.
2. *Ibid.*, p. 3.
3. Seamus Heaney, 'The New Poet Laureate', in Leonard M. Scigaj (ed.), *Critical Essays on Ted Hughes* (New York: G. K. Hall, 1992), p. 46.
4. *Ibid.*, p. 46.
5. Roberts, pp. 5, 4.
6. John Bayley, 'Godmother of the Salmon', review of *Rain-Charm for the Duchy and other Laureate Poems*, *London Review of Books* 9 July 1992, p. 9.

Works Cited

Hughes's Poetry

The Hawk in the Rain London: Faber, 1957.
Lupercal London: Faber, 1960.
Wodwo London: Faber, 1967.
Crow: From the Life and Songs of the Crow London: Faber, 1970, 1972.
Gaudete London: Faber, 1977.
Cave Birds: An Alchemical Cave Drama with drawings by Leonard Baskin, London: Faber, 1978.
Moortown London: Faber, 1979.
Remains of Elmet: A Pennine Sequence with photographs by Fay Godwin, London: Faber, 1979.
Selected Poems 1957–1981 London: Faber, 1982.
River with photographs by Peter Keen, London: Faber, 1983.
Flowers and Insects Some Birds and a Pair of Spiders with drawings by Leonard Baskin, London: Faber, 1986.
Wolfwatching London: Faber, 1989.
Rain-Charm for the Duchy and other Laureate Poems London: Faber, 1992.
New Selected Poems 1957–1994 London: Faber, 1995.

By Ted Hughes: non-fictional prose, interviews and recordings

'The Rock', *The Listener* vol. 70, 19 September 1963, pp. 421–423.
Poetry in the Making: An Anthology of Poems and Programmes from 'Listening and Writing' London: Faber, 1967.
'The chronological order of Sylvia Plath's poems', in Charles Newman (ed.), *The Art of Sylvia Plath: A Symposium* London: Faber, 1970.
'Ted Hughes's *Crow*', *The Listener* vol. 84, 30 July 1970, p. 149.

'Myth and Education', *Children's Literature in Education* 1, 1970, pp. 55–70.

'Ted Hughes and *Crow*', Interview with Ted Hughes, by Ekbert Faas, *London Magazine* vol. 10 no. 10, January 1971, pp. 5–20.

Unpublished letter to Neil Roberts and Terry Gifford, October 1978.

'Ted Hughes and *Gaudete*', Interview with Ted Hughes, in Ekbert Faas, *Ted Hughes: The Unaccommodated Universe* Santa Barbara: Black Sparrow, 1980.

'Five Poems by Ted Hughes', written and presented by Ted Hughes, for 'The English Programme', Thames Television, 1989.

'A Reply to Critics' and 'On Images in *Crow*', in A. E. Dyson (ed.), *Three Contemporary Poets: Thom Gunn, Ted Hughes and R. S. Thomas: A Casebook* Basingstoke: Macmillan, 1990.

A Dancer to God: Tributes to T. S. Eliot London: Faber, 1992.

Shakespeare and the Goddess of Complete Being London: Faber, 1992.

Interview with Ted Hughes, by Clive Wilmer, *P. N. Review* vol. 19 no. 3, Jan–Feb. 1993, pp. 36–38.

Winter Pollen: Occasional Prose ed. William Scammell, London: Faber, 1994.

Criticism on Hughes

Bayley, John 'Godmother of the Salmon', review of *Rain-Charm for the Duchy and other Laureate Poems, London Review of Books* 9 July 1992, pp. 9–10.

Bedient, Calvin *Eight Contemporary Poets* London: Oxford University Press, 1974.

Eagleton, Terry review of *Gaudete, Stand* vol. 19 no. 2, 1978, pp. 76–80.

Fuller, Roy 'Views', *The Listener* vol. 85, 11 March 1971, pp. 296–297.

Gifford, Terry and Roberts, Neil *Ted Hughes: A Critical Study* London: Faber, 1981.

Heaney, Seamus 'The New Poet Laureate', in Leonard M. Scigaj (ed.), *Critical Essays on Ted Hughes* New York: G. K. Hall, 1992.

Hirschberg, Stuart *Myth in the Poetry of Ted Hughes* Dublin: Wolfhound Press, 1981.

Lodge, David *Working with Structuralism: Essays and Reviews on Nineteenth- and Twentieth-Century Literature* London: Routledge, 1981.

Lucas, John 'The exclusive eye', review of *Wolfwatching* and *Moortown Diary, TLS* October 20–26, 1989, p. 1148.

Raban, Jonathan *The Society of the Poem* London: Harrap, 1971.

Roberts, Neil 'Hughes, Narrative, and Lyric: An Analysis of *Gaudete*', in Keith Sagar (ed.), *The Challenge of Ted Hughes* Basingstoke: Macmillan, 1994.

Roberts, Neil 'Ted Hughes and the Laureateship', *Critical Quarterly* vol. 27 no. 2, summer 1985, pp. 3–5.

Robinson, Craig *Ted Hughes as Shepherd of Being* Basingstoke: Macmillan, 1989.

Sagar, Keith *The Art of Ted Hughes* second edition, Cambridge: Cambridge University Press, 1978.

Scigaj, Leonard M. *The Poetry of Ted Hughes: Form and Imagination* Iowa: Iowa University Press, 1986.

Scigaj, Leonard M. *Ted Hughes* Boston: G. K. Hall, 1991.

Sweeting, Michael 'Hughes and Shamanism', in Keith Sagar (ed.), *The Achievement of Ted Hughes* Manchester: Manchester University Press, 1983.

Thurley, Geoffrey *The Ironic Harvest: English Poetry in the Twentieth Century* London: Arnold, 1974.

West, Thomas *Ted Hughes* London: Methuen, 1985.

Other Works Cited

Bakhtin, Mikhail *Rabelais and his World* trans. Hélène Iswolsky, Cambridge, Mass.: MIT Press, 1968.

Bakhtin, Mikhail *The Dialogic Imagination: Four Essays by M. M. Bakhtin* ed. Michael Holquist, trans. Caryl Emerson and Michael Holquist, Austin: University of Texas Press, 1981.

Bakhtin, Mikhail *Problems of Dostoevsky's Poetics* ed. and trans. Caryl Emerson, Manchester: Manchester University Press, 1984.

Barthes, Roland *Camera Lucida: Reflections on Photography* trans. Richard Howard, London: Fontana, 1984.

Barthes, Roland *A Lover's Discourse: Fragments* trans. Richard Howard, London: Penguin, 1990.

Barthes, Roland *The Pleasure of the Text* trans. Richard Howard, Oxford: Blackwell, 1990.

Barthes, Roland *Roland Barthes* trans. Richard Howard, London: Papermac, 1995.

Conquest, Robert (ed.) *New Lines: An Anthology* London: Macmillan, 1956.

Eliade, Mircea *Shamanism: Archaic Techniques of Ecstasy* trans. Willard R. Trask, London: Routledge, 1964.

Graves, Robert *The White Goddess: A Historical Grammar of Poetic Myth* amended edition, London: Faber, 1961.

Haffenden, John *Viewpoints: Poets in Conversation with John Haffenden* London: Faber, 1981.

Jung, C. G. *Memories, Dreams, Reflections* recorded and ed. Anelia Jaffé, trans. Richard and Clara Winston, London: Flamingo, 1983.

Jung, C. G. 'On the Psychology of the Trickster Figure', in Paul Radin, *The Trickster: A Study in American Indian Mythology* New York: Schocken, 1972.

Jung, C. G. *Psychology and Alchemy* second edition, trans. R. F. C. Hull, London: Routledge, 1968.

Kristeva, Julia *Black Sun: Depression and Melancholia* trans. Leon S. Roudiez, New York: Columbia University Press, 1989.

Kristeva, Julia *Desire in Language: A Semiotic Approach to Literature and Art* ed. Leon S. Roudiez, trans. Thomas Gora, Alice Jardine and Leon S. Roudiez, Oxford: Blackwell, 1981.

Kristeva, Julia *The Kristeva Reader* ed. Toril Moi, Oxford: Blackwell, 1986.

Kristeva, Julia *Tales of Love* trans. Leon S. Roudiez, New York: Columbia University Press, 1987.

Kristeva, Julia 'Talking about *Polylogue*', in Toril Moi (ed.), *French Feminist Thought: A Reader* Oxford: Blackwell, 1987.

Lacan, Jacques *Écrits: A Selection* trans. Alan Sheridan, London: Tavistock/Routledge, 1977.

Lacan, Jacques *The Four Fundamental Concepts of Psychoanalysis* ed. Jacques-Alain Miller, trans. Alan Sheridan, London: Penguin, 1977.

Lacan, Jacques *The Seminar of Jacques Lacan Book I. Freud's Papers on Technique 1953–1954* ed. Jacques-Alain Miller, trans. John Forrester, Cambridge: Cambridge University Press, 1988.

Lacan, Jacques *The Seminar of Jacques Lacan Book II. The Ego in Freud's Theory and in the Technique of Psychoanalysis 1954–1955* ed. Jacques-Alain Miller, trans. Sylvana Tomaselli, Cambridge: Cambridge University Press, 1988.

Lacan, Jacques 'Of Structure as an Inmixing of Otherness Prerequisite to Any Subject Whatever', in Richard Macksey and Eugenio Donato (eds), *The Structuralist Controversy: The Languages of Criticism and the Sciences of Man* London: Johns Hopkins University Press, 1970.

Laplanche, J., Pontalis, J.-B. *The Language of Psycho-Analysis* trans. Donald Nicholson-Smith, London: Karnac, 1988.

Lévi-Strauss, Claude *Structural Anthropology* trans. Claire Jacobson and Brooke Grundfest Schoepf, London: Penguin, 1963.

Oliver, Kelly *Reading Kristeva: Unraveling the Double-bind* Bloomington: Indiana University Press, 1993.

Plath, Sylvia *Collected Poems* ed. Ted Hughes, London: Faber, 1981.

Radin, Paul *The Trickster: A Study in American Indian Mythology* New York: Schocken, 1972.

Rose, Jacqueline *The Haunting of Sylvia Plath* London: Virago, 1991.

Shelley, Percy Bysshe 'To a Skylark', in Duncan Wu (ed.), *Romanticism: An Anthology* Oxford: Blackwell, 1994.

Smith, A. C. H. *Orghast at Persepolis* London: Methuen, 1972.

Vendler, Helen *The Music of What Happens: Poems, Poets, Critics* Cambridge, Mass.: Harvard University Press, 1988.

Wehr, Demaris *Jung and Feminism: Liberating Archetypes* London: Routledge, 1988.

Wordsworth, William 'I Wandered Lonely as a Cloud', in Harold Bloom and Lionel Trilling (eds), *Romantic Poetry and Prose* Oxford: Oxford University Press, 1973.

Wordsworth, William *The Prelude*, in Duncan Wu (ed.), *Romanticism: An Anthology* Oxford: Blackwell, 1994.

Index